Claire Underwood '88. Bought '87.



GIRLS ARE POWERFUL

CLAIRE'S COS SHE IS COOL!

But, cool (?) Claire, I've read it as well and as far the title, well I'm powerful, more than you anyway!!

# GIRLS ARE POWERFUL

## Young women's writings from Spare Rib

Sheba Feminist Publishers 1982

Girls Are Powerful first published in Great Britain in April 1982 by Sheba Feminist Publishers, 488 Kingsland Road, London E8.

Acknowledgement is gratefully made to the authors for permission to reprint their work.

Designed by Pat Kahn
ISBN: 0 907179 12 6
Photoset in Univers Light at Range Left
Printed and bound by A. Wheaton & Co Ltd Exeter

## *Contents*

The work of putting the collection together is dedicated to the editor's daughter Lisa Bahaire, and to Natasha Spedding, Kelly Kennedy and Anna Winter.

# *Editor's preface*

***Spare Rib*** is a women's liberation magazine. It comes out monthly, and is usually on sale alongside (maybe rather tucked behind!) other magazines for women, in the newsagents.

We don't have an over-all editor. We work as a group, a collective of women, sharing the work and the decisions. We aim to cover topics that concern and interest women, from a perspective which doesn't get much airing in other publications, and that means we have a policy of printing pieces by those groups of women who hardly ever get a say anywhere else.

Take young women, for example. There are many magazines produced commercially ***for*** them, but, apart from a few letters, there is hardly ever anything ***by*** them inside. More and more young women have become really angry at the way such magazines presume they are all brainless and passive, interested only in fashion and getting a boyfriend . . . and ready to ditch their girl friends in the scramble. Serious topics rarely get discussed.

Ironically, there's another area in which young women have had very little say – in the growing volume of feminist research on young women's lives at school and in youth clubs. This work has done wonders in opening many people's minds to the ways in which girls are disadvantaged, but it hasn't so far allowed ***them*** to describe and analyse their experiences.

In this collection, the pieces are by young women of seven to 22, with one or two exceptions. They have mainly been published in ***Spare Rib*** over the past seven years, and there are some pieces, too, from ***Shocking Pink***, the magazine written and brought out by young women.

At *Spare Rib*, our ages range from 22 to 41, and we intend the magazine to reach a wide range of readership. So we know that the young women's pieces we publish do not cover all the things they might like to say if they were writing just for themselves, or in a context where a collective of older women did not take the main editorial decisions.

We are bringing out this book to give all these pieces a place together, in a way which we hope will emphasise the strength of what they have to say. We would like it to be read widely by girls and young women. But it's also meant for all of us who are no longer that age, because too often we disregard their ideas, feeling they are too young to teach us anything. It's a document to prove us wrong – girls are powerful!

*Susan Hemmings*
Spare Rib *Collective*
*London 1982*

PENNY SILLIN
Walking about, you see such a lot of creeps.... especially on the tube— all those smug execs in their suits, or the snooty assistants from Horrids....
EMBANKMENT
bark
Will passengers PLEASE mind the gap and STAND CLEAR of the DOORS!!
oink!
Still, today I've decided to wake their ideas up a bit....strike a blow at conformity!
TIMES
tch! Youth of today...no wonder this country's going to the dogs!
probably another scrounger on the dole... should bring back National Service and send the foreigners back where they came from
fury
TIMES
god! Doesn't she look unfeminine...!
Lounge
Humph! How dog-ist
Bitches Lib
Suddenly...
SPLAT!
SPLURGE!
SPLOSH!
QUICK EXIT
It's getting a bit hairy in this cartoon
You too can be a secretary
underneath they're all loveable
Don't pick your nose
The tube's pretty dehumanising.. just look at all these robots going down the conveyor belt
Please stand on right
Phew! Oo look, some normal people
LITTE
(overhears conversation)
Pulled a new bird last night in the pub—she was a bit of alright
oh yeh?
GRRRRR!
The creeps are everywhere!
You don't have to be THAT normal!
LITTER
NORMAL??? Bang goes my street credibility
sue.

# LOOKS

## *Bovver boots and eyeliner*

I have been a punk(ette??) for some time now and I wear plenty of black eyeliner and bright eye-shadow. Am I wrong? *I* don't think so. I support the women's movement with fervour but I do feel that I should be able to wear make-up if I like.

Female punks are not the most 'feminine' people you've ever set eyes on. I (and mes amies) don't want to look all pretty-pretty. Jeans and Doc Marten's boots are lots more comfortable than tights and a flimsy wee skirt! In a way though I contradict myself by wearing coloured stuff on my face. This is wrong because I am being monopolised by the people who make you feel that you must be beautiful for the men in our society. Posters and TV commercials shout at us from every angle, 'Buy new Wonder Lash and you'll be a star overnight'. But then I simply do not look like a model. My make-up isn't meant to flatter me!

My reason for wearing make-up is simply that *I* like it and it's fun doing experiments on your face. If you're depressed, make-up is one form of release, too. It's a laugh and experimenting with it can lead to an entirely new appearance – if that's what you want. I believe that you should only do what ***you*** want to ***your*** face – it does not belong to anyone else. Of course, the same applies if you don't want to wear make-up, after all it's only decoration. Make-up is generally used to attract attention. Shame that it sometimes works in the wrong way.

Almost everyone knows what it's like to be shouted at in the street – it can be very hurtful. Isn't it funny (no, it's to be expected) that females generally are on the receiving end of the hurled abuse? It's my theory that many men are frightened of other males; fewer remarks are made about male punks, mods, boyfriends, husbands, rockers, skins, teds and so on. Could this be fear of getting involved in a fight? Men realise that most women will not stand up to them so they can get away with it.

I've had so many arguments with blokes about my eye make-up (I don't generally wear any other kind). How do you tell a guy who is about as broad-minded as a cold chip that it's nothing to do with him what you do to your face? They just sit there and once you've shot your mouth off efficiently (***you*** think) they turn round and say – 'But ***I*** don't like it'! Ever felt like wringing someone's neck?

Obviously many people think that it's not up to the individual to do what they want to their faces. I'm sure that many young women (and maybe some boys) have been called into the head teacher's room because he or she does not like the appearance of the pupil. When our headmaster told me to clean that 'stuff' off my eyes during lunchtime, he also said that as head of the school he could have authority over ***my*** face. I left his office feeling really furious and humiliated.

But for all the shit and abuse I've heard and put

up with – I'm still going to wear make-up. Lots of people have been reconciled to the fact that if *I* want to wear it, I'm bloody well going to!! Whatever happens, even an anti-capitalist revolution, I think that make-up will always be used and I'm glad. It's a great way of doing something different – however outrageous to some narrow-minded person – I hope it stays that way. Bovver boots and eyeliner rool OK!

*Mairi Damer*

# *One small horrid word*

*Dear Spare Rib,*

Every time I buy ***Spare Rib***, I immediately look for the health article, in the hope of finding that ***this*** month it will at last reassure me that I am not the only one.

That it isn't just me who is recoiled from (that it isn't just me who imagines she is recoiled from?).

– That it isn't just me who is in constant physical pain.

– That it isn't just me who 'blows it up out of all proportion'.

– That it isn't just me who makes regular, embarrassing trips to the doctor.

– That it isn't just me who cringes every time certain everyday words are spoken at home, school, on TV, film . . . complexion, skin, smooth, healthy glow, soft . . .

– That it isn't just me who has tried every product on the market.

– That it isn't just me who is unable to look people in the eye.

– That it isn't just me who feels utterly ashamed because, although an ardent feminist, I recourse to mascara and make-up.

– That it isn't just me who feels so ugly, inadequate and completely weary that nothing can be done to help . . .

I fear so much that you will all find it foolish, please don't. The word is ***acne***. The courage it has taken me to say it, to 'admit' it! If only that would exorcise it! But no – it doesn't. Nothing does. Please believe me, it is isolation. It is hell. And it is made so much worse by your never writing an article about it – for that is indicative of your thinking it a minor problem, insignificant, trivial.

May I show you that you are wrong? Next time you see one of us with acne, do not say, 'I used to be spotty until I . . .', or 'Don't worry, you'll grow out of it', or 'Have you tried . . .?'

Please:

1. Appreciate that the sufferer will have tried: Clearasil, witch hazel, Phisohex, Phisoderm, Phisomel, medicated soaps, Topex, TCP, face packs, Swiss bio-facial, Neutrogena, DDD, Valderma, Torbetol, Quinoderm, antibiotics, Neomedrone, Actinac, Toracsol, Dome-acne, white spirit. They all work for a while, but soon lose their effectiveness. Then there's the side effects of papery, tender eyelids, chapped lips, dried hands . . .

2. Appreciate the joy of washing your face, neck, chest, back and not feeling dozens of lumps, bumps, ridges, holes . . .

3. Appreciate the joy of not dying inside when your lover runs his hand over your skin and finds to his consternation . . .

4. Appreciate the joy of not feeling everyone thinks you can't be clean, or careful.

I am a vegetarian.
I do eat health foods.
I am clean.
I never eat chocolate, chips, ice-cream, licorice, rich or spicy foods, though I like them.
I do take a lot of exercise.
I have plenty of rest and fresh air.
I never touch my spots.
I always use a clean towel, pillow case, tie my hair back.
I know it's hormonal! I know it's nervous!

But if you have acne, you feel that people think you ***can*** help it, and/or that they are repelled. And who can blame them? One is so repelled by oneself. It's just impossible ***not*** to be disgusted by endless greasiness, pus, scars – will you even print these ugly words I wonder?

Readers, before you condemn me as unliberated or vain or self-pitying or pathetic for being so affected by my acne (honestly, I wish I did regard it as insignificant, compared to all the atrocities being committed all over the world), believe me: I don't need to be pretty, nor to have an 'attractive' body. I just wish I could do something about this acne which *hurts* me so much as it destroys the tissues of my skin, and which twists me inside as it destroys my self-regard, my confidence, my peace of mind, and worst of all, my love for my normal-skinned sisters.

Thank you for listening. I'm sorry I can't sign my name on this article.

*An unknown woman*

## *Letters came pouring in . . .*

*Dear Unknown Woman,*

Having just read your letter in *Spare Rib* after a hard day, I felt compelled to write to you. Your letter speaks for me, too. Since the age of twelve, the onset of my periods, I have had acne. I was told that it would soon pass. I am now nineteen and although there is an improvement, it certainly hasn't gone.

Growing up hasn't been much fun at all during my school years, being called 'spotty', 'ugly' etc until it got to the point where I couldn't look at anyone. I had one friend with whom I didn't feel embarrassed, and she was the only person who understood how hurt and embarrassed I really felt. Now, however, I do find it easier to talk about it to other women and to actually ask them what they feel about acne. Surprisingly most of them are not bothered; some say it doesn't notice when you like someone.

I still can't help but think they can never understand how much it can screw you up. It's all very well for some women to say you're self-pitying, but it's much deeper than that. It's not as if you're asking to be Raquel Welch – you're asking just to be able to look at people with some confidence, to talk, to laugh without feeling so self-conscious.

Anyway, please write, and I can write a longer letter. Bye for now. ***M***.

*Dear Spare Rib*,

I felt I had to write in response to the Unknown Woman.

I started with my affliction at a very early and horrifying age – eleven years old, a time which is vitally important in one's life. Before 'acne' I was a happy, contented, reasonably well-balanced person. I am now 21, and it is still with me, and it is only recently that I have been able to come anywhere near able to cope with it.

Like your reader, I have tried endless remedies, and made endless trips to doctors, hospitals, dermatologists, beauticians (yuk), etc etc with little or no effect. My worst experience ever was a visit to a beauty salon in Manchester (very reputable!) when I was about sixteen years old. I was lain down on a bed – all protective layers (make-up) stripped off – you just can't imagine the vulnerability – and then a cluster of petite, ultra-feminine, sweet-smelling, perfect-skinned, newly-engaged trainees all peered at me, prodding and poking my stricken face. I began to sob hysterically, and they all said how sorry they felt. At that moment I wanted to take a knife and cut up every one of their faces.

One of my major problems in adolescence was that of feeling 'no one will ever love me'. I have never been closer to suicide than when, at eighteen, a three year relationship was ended by my partner. Suicide has been contemplated many times, usually after one of my self-persecution sessions. I would wash and sit in bed with the light on and bring a magnifying mirror right up to my face. Then I would cry and scream for hours. I have now learned to avoid mirrors at all costs. Many times I have emerged from dressing rooms in shops in tears without even trying on the garment. The sight of my own horrific face in the mirror would be enough to once again convince me that I could never look nice in anything.

I used to be a really good swimmer at school. Everyone said I could have been better, but it got so that I couldn't bear to go – guess why. The water would wash off all my make up, and worse – everyone would see the spots on my back. More restrictions include:

1. Never going in places with bright lights – hating going shopping.

2. Dreading going to discos, because the lights might suddenly come on at the end of the night.

3. Crossing my legs for hours when I'm out drinking or socialising because I can't bear to go to the 'ladies', as when I get there I might have to pass a brightly-lit mirror, usually clustered round with nice-skinned people.

4. Never being able to go on holidays like camping, or stay at a friend's unexpectedly, because I may not be able to attend to my face properly or I may not have my stuff with me.

The list is literally endless!

I feel I must stop this letter now – I could go on for ever – I've always said to my mother that perhaps one day I'd write a book about it, but who would want to read about spots? Anyway, I do hope the anonymous woman becomes unanonymous. I'd like her to know she's not the only one. *L.*

**LOOKS 8**

## *Unknown woman now replies . . .*

*Dear Sisters,*

I read with indescribable relief and gratitude all your helpful, trusting and empathetic letters to my anonymous article on acne. I only wish you could all read each other's letters, to support you too. But, what can we ***do***? There were a few suggestions of cures that I haven't actually tried, would you believe – and of course I view them with great wariness, but of course I shall try them . . . However, just in case they don't work (ha ha) I'm writing this to encourage and reassure other women (quick thank you to 'Jim' from London who also took the trouble to write) with acne, who haven't yet got the confidence to contact anyone about their anxiety, self-hatred and fears.

A lovely lady who wrote to me suggested it: could we not form some sort of group to enable us to share our experiences, and get the best out of medical help?

I'd really love to hear from anyone who is suffering in anguished silence, and will reply personally with, hopefully, contact from others like us – it was certainly a tremendous help to me – and makes a nice change from being advised to 'purify the blood' with rhubarb, or to get pregnant!

Feminists of the world unite, you have nothing to lose but your spots!

*Love and sisterhood*
*Kathryn Johnson.*

Cindy
AFTER LEAVING RODNEY AND HER LUXURIOUS LIFE BEHIND, CINDY ARRIVES IN LONDON TO MAKE A FRESH START IN LIFE AND CONTACT BIONIC WOMAN — . .
LONDON! THIS IS WHERE IT ALL HAPPENS!
I CAN BE FREE TO CHOOSE —
MAKE A FRESH START . . . .
IT WAS OK AT FIRST AND THEN AS I KEPT ON DRIVING ROUND I SLOWLY STARTED TO FEEL SMALL AND . . . . .
I WAS JUST BEGINNING TO GET REALLY PISSED OFF, WHEN I SUDDENLY SAW A NOISY GANG OF WOMEN IN A 'HOT ROD' CAR. (NOT UNLIKE MY OWN.) ⇨
GREAT COINCIDENCE ON THE WAY!!

IT WAS 'BIONIC WOMEN' AND SOME FRIENDS—
HEY!
A COUPLE OF DRINKS LATER I WAS BEGINNING TO FEEL MUCH BETTER—
THE 'MENSTRALS' ARE PLAYING TONIGHT. WHY DONT WE GO?
I'M REALLY ENJOYING BEING WITH YOU ALL!
" OF COURSE HE DIDN'T REALIZE I WAS A BLACKBELT.
JUST WAIT THIS IS ONLY THE BEGINNING
AND A GREAT TIME WAS HAD BY ALL!!
NELLY SPIT AND SUE BONG

# *The trouble with trousers . . .*

The problem at Isabel, Jayne and Sylvia's junior school is basically with a very strict headmistress who doesn't like girls in trousers. If they wear them, she gives them a good telling off. When common sense prevailed on her to let them wear them through the snow to school, she still insisted that when they arrived they had to change into skirts. And if it was ***very*** cold in school, they could wear the trousers . . . with a skirt over them!

Most of the teachers at this junior school are women, and they wear trousers. They don't want to tell the girls off, but ***they'll*** get into trouble if they don't make them change. And most of the mothers, too, like their girls in trousers at home, and don't really see why they shouldn't wear them to school, but definitely don't want their girls breaking school rules.

One day this October, Isabel, Jayne and Sylvia decided enough was enough, and made a plan with their friends to all turn up in trousers the next day. They all had sleepless nights worrying if the others would be able to and, sure enough, several parents put a stop to it. Still, those three and a couple of others managed to wear them, and two of them kept them on all day. 'At lunch time we felt really sick, because the head walks about then and can see us. We kept behind the other girls. Other children kept saying to us, "Why are you wearing them? Are we allowed?" And we said, "We want to". The thing is, everyone is so scared of getting into trouble. Lots of them agree with us – but they won't take the risk of getting told off.' It is difficult in junior schools – especially for the fourth (final) year students, whose behaviour record goes forward to secondary school and might affect their chances there.

They don't dislike wearing skirts. 'But you can't do so many things in them. You can't run or climb, because you have to wear special shoes with skirts, you can't just wear plimsolls. Skirts blow around in the playground, and the boys are always lifting them up. In trousers you can sit more comfortably on the floor. Your legs are protected when you fall over. You are generally much freer.' They've been told that if they wore trousers, they'd get the hems wet on the toilet floors . . . and that they'd get sweaty . . . 'Well, if all those things are true, boys should wear shorts.'

In any case they don't agree with being told what to wear. 'They're just trying to get us trained for when we have to wear uniform at secondary school and we don't agree with that either. It's got nothing to do with what you learn or how you behave.' They are considering ways to get more support for their trousers protest, especially from mothers and teachers. 'Even people who don't want us to break rules should see that it's a nonsense rule, and if they don't want it broken, it should be changed.'

When the cold weather started last year – and it ***was*** extremely cold – school students at East Barnet Comprehensive School decided they'd had enough, and organised an extensive trousers protest, perhaps the biggest yet. It started with a petition, which built support among the fourth, fifth and sixth year students, getting about 300 signatures. Because so many students, both girls and boys, were interested, they decided to hold a meeting at which they planned 'four days of action', and started a National Union of School Students branch. The first day some of the boys came in wearing skirts, and lots of girls wore trousers. The boys were made to change, but the girls weren't – that day.

During the afternoon the head circulated a message that the NUSS had called off the trousers protest, which they hadn't. Students were meeting all over the school, feeling they were winning, and that they didn't want to call it off. The next day 150 girls came in trousers, and now the trouble began. The boy the head thought was the ringleader was called in. 'We think perhaps you ought to go home for a little while . . .' 'Do you mean I'm being suspended?' 'Well . . . yes, I suppose so.' But as he went out into the school entrance hall, many other students, especially fifth year girls, came out to support him. A teacher asked them to return: 'Are you with the school or with your union?' 'We're with our union,' they replied, and before long about 50 of them were picketing the school gates, on strike. The police came, so after a while they decided to go to a neighbouring college to hold another meeting . . . and the bus was followed all the way by the police. At the college, they made leaflets, to explain their protest to their own school and to others, and they decided to meet the next morning early, and resume the picket. Next day 80 students were still on strike on the gate, and girls trying to get into school in trousers were not allowed in. The head began sending out letters to all their parents telling them their children were off school . . . even when many were ***trying*** to get in, but banned because they had trousers on.

This pressure, and the hassling by the police following them to and from the college where they went to meet, finally brought it all to a close. Looking back on it now, they think they made a good protest, even though it came to nothing, because it involved so many students. But next time they'll structure it more carefully, with proper representatives from each year, and an elected strike committee, dividing the work of petitioning, leafleting and picketing, as well as publicity, so that it doesn't all fall on one or two people who get the main brunt of the blame. It's amazing to think that students have been petitioning, persuading, and now taking strike action at this school every year for ***seven*** years, and they've still got nowhere . . . shows you how determined some authority figures are to keep girls in their place!

. well, I understand you feel, Mrs. Jones, I do like my girls to like girls, and trousers so <u>dirty</u> in the ground."

Sheila Sen writes from Scotland: I have always been anti-racist, because my mother is white and my father is Black. It wasn't until I got to secondary school, and came up against sexism first hand, that I started to want to fight against that, too. One thing which I wanted to make a protest about was that girls are not allowed to wear trousers.

I took the most direct, but probably not the best, approach, simply going to school in trousers, blatantly breaking the rules, so I'd be sent to the headteacher and given the chance to explain. I got a lift into school, so I didn't meet anyone I knew until I went to my first class, chemistry, taught by the seniors' headmaster. As I was already late, he was already angry. (I'm always late in the mornings and I'm sure that he's drawn proof of delinquent tendencies from this.) I remember he was leaning over a bunsen burner when he noticed me. 'Trousers, Sheila?' I go red. ' . . .Yes.' I don't think he expected me to have thought about what I was doing. When I argued back and explained that I thought girls should be able to, he seemed very surprised. After a mumbled lecture he sent me to the head guidance teacher . . . and so it went on. Passing the buck. I still don't know how I got the courage, because I'm not a particularly confident person, especially when faced with people who could expel me.

They decided I would have to be sent home. But first they gave me an early pass for school dinner, which I thought was really funny, them being concerned that I was well-fed before they threatened me with expulsion. And they asked me to try not to be too noticeable, in case it 'gave other girls ideas'.

When I got home, we all sat around the kitchen table and my parents asked me all about it. My dad seemed quite understanding, but my mum just didn't see the point in it, and still doesn't, because I'll be leaving school soon and 'a good character report goes a long way towards getting into college'.

Anyway, the mild fuss it caused didn't do anything to change matters. So a few days later I posted petitions up in all the girls' cloakrooms – and gathered a disgusting six signatures from about 700 girls. I put the petitions up at the suggestion of a male teacher who said to do that and then go directly to the school board with them to make a protest. He said that he couldn't help because he was a teacher, and I think he would have got into trouble if he had.

About a day later they were taken down. Another teacher told me something I think is true – that the other girls just weren't bothered enough to risk being branded 'troublemakers'. Although I didn't exactly lose any friends at this point, I didn't gain any support, either.

My headmaster hasn't spoken to me about it since, but he makes it clear that he hasn't forgotten. My mother's still worried for my future, and my 'Fight Sexism in Schools' badge tends to agitate the stricter teachers. Being sixteen means you have a certain amount of freedom compared to younger students, but apparently free speech isn't a part of it. Fight sexism in schools? Damn right we will!

Catherine Mahony is seven, and stopped wearing trousers about three years ago – except for very limited occasions.

'The only rule for us is you're not allowed to wear too high heels because you do a lot of running around. And they don't really want you to wear very long dresses. I find dresses or skirts the most comfortable to wear – trousers I find too tight up here and round here (tummy and thighs). All my friends wear skirts. Dungarees aren't too tight, but it takes a long time to alter the straps, either too tight or too low, and you can spend all day altering them.

'I have to wear trousers when I'm painting. I forget all about them then. When I was painting that wall I splashed paint all over them, and if I'd been wearing a dress it would have gone all over the dress and all over my legs. And if you know you're going to do an enormous amount of climbing, like going up Snowdon, then you should wear them. Or at the park (though I don't wear them, because I don't want to keep changing). My sister dropped her chewing gum over the railings when she went up the park, so she stood on the top, went to jump down, but fell down and tore all her skirt. She wasn't wearing trousers that time.

'People say that girls should only wear skirts, because it's not fair if girls can wear skirts and trousers and boys can only wear trousers. And sometimes you're walking around outside school and you hear parents saying, there's something wrong with that school because there are girls wearing trousers. And one of my friends' mothers says, "I don't want my girl wearing trousers because they are for boys." And I think some girls do worry that if they wear trousers people will think they are not proper girls. I don't worry about that though. I just don't feel comfortable in them.

'If I was playing football, I'd wear trousers. But I find it too rough, because they kick the ball so hard I can't run fast enough. I think when parents have boys they train them to be rougher because they think boys should be stronger than girls.

'I wear my track suit trousers sometimes, like for long walks in the country. I didn't want to, we had a row, but now I think they're quite comfortable. And the same with pyjama trousers – I refused to, we had a fight, then I was really surprised how comfortable they were, and when I grew out of them, I was upset and wanted another pair like them. It's important for me to try to get used to trousers, though. Because there may be a point where you have to wear skirts, and there may be a point where you have to wear trousers. Like for rope climbing – I went in a skirt, and I was very lucky I didn't get it torn. So it's best to get used to wearing both. But what I don't like is that they're loose at the bottom and tight at the top . . .'

# AT SCHOOL

## *She must be a women's libber!*

Here's a typical school day.

As I walk to the station to catch the train to school, I pass the same set of adverts, with photographs of women models, showing off their long legs, and pictures of hunky men showing what their right arm is for.

I sit in the train glancing at my neighbour's magazine, and read ***be*** like so and so, and ***do*** such and such to myself, and ***wear*** a particular lipstick to have all the boys come and kiss me.

I go to an all girls' school. At our assembly in the morning the headmistress announces that our netball team has lost 23-0 to another school and concludes, 'Both teams played well.' The point that we have no constructive criticism is put to a few teachers by some of us. We point out that our brother school has criticism of this kind and that seems to be beneficial. 'Oh, but girls would be upset by that', is the answer.

My friend and I try to bring up the subject of stereotyping of girls in a discussion. The other girls refuse to believe that they shave their legs and wear mascara and want to marry as soon as possible for fear of becoming old maids, as a result of conditioning. Even the teacher refuses to accept our arguments. My friend and I feel utterly alone in our anger at society's view of females.

There's the inevitable discusson at break about what eye shadow so-and-so wears, and sniggers that what's-her-name doesn't wear a bra. 'She must be a women's libber!' I show them ***Spare Rib***. They flick through it and say, 'Where's the John Travolta pin-up?' They show me their magazines in a tone that suggests that I should be humoured, tell me that I can take them home to read, and see what I should do with my hair and skin, and what clothes to buy to be fashionable. I ***just*** keep my temper, decline to read them, and walk away.

Then at home the struggle continues. I have to help my mother (who works full-time as a nursery nurse) get through the housework when she gets home, while my father watches the television. If I remark on this I get a lecture based on the sixth commandment, 'honour thy father and mother . . .'

I've practically given up watching television. The majority of the programmes subtly tell me how I should behave to make a success of my life, and make me sick. Instead I curl up in bed with ***Spare Rib*** or a recommended (feminist) book.

And so endeth another day.

*Viv Norman*

# To school with fear

I ask myself, what is it about it? And I'm not the only one, you know. Many people feel like me. But I can't keep going, not when you hear all the things they're saying to you every day. Then, you know, two people will have a fight and it will never end, and everybody round it is part of it. If you want one person to win and you tell this to the wrong person then you lose some more friends. It keeps going like this too. It's not only Black against white, but mostly that's what it is. That seems to be all that's happening in school these days. You can't tell the teachers about it. Of course they know, but if you tell them, the other kids think you're weak, or scared, or not loyal to them. No one is allowed to tell anybody they're afraid. I tell my best friend Jessie, but I wouldn't tell anybody else. Some days I get so scared before I have to go to school I feel like I'm going to, you know, throw up. I run into the bathroom but nothing happens. I know it won't because it's nerves.

Every day I walk by this long brick wall. You have to go through this little passage way to get to school. There's usually a cat there climbing around. When I see him I tell him, 'Bring me good luck.' He usually runs away, which I tell myself is a good sign. Then I tell myself, 'No matter what anybody tells you, don't be upset, don't be afraid.' Sometimes it works, but most of the time it doesn't, especially if Jessie isn't with me. It's better when she's with me. I'd rather have someone yell out, 'There goes two nigger girls', than have me be there all by myself. You don't know what they're going to do next when they do it, and it's always happening. You don't know what's the best thing to do either. Like they'll say, 'Hey, you short nigger, what are you, some kind of a pygmy?' That's my own special name because I'm short. Aren't they clever! I never know what to do. Some people say, 'You shout back at them so they won't do it again.' But I couldn't get myself to do that. What am I supposed to do when it happens, like, when we're on the playground or the stairs? Or in the class too? It happens in class too. 'Hey pygmy, you read the lesson for today?' What am I supposed to do? Jessie says I should keep my mouth shut and tell one of the boys, like, the biggest person I see, 'That kid over there called me a pygmy.' That's what she says to do because she says if we don't start fighting back they'll never stop doing it to us. Maybe she's right, but I can't see myself going up to some guy and telling him what someone said to me.

The boys tell us too, to tell them. They say they'll go after anyone we want them to, that they're not afraid of a single person in the school. I can't believe what's going on. If you tell someone, you don't know what kind of trouble you may be starting, and if you keep your mouth shut, you know what you're letting go on. But everyone keeps saying, 'They aren't going to hurt you, nothing will happen.' But I don't see why they should be allowed to call me things that has to do with my being coloured, and that's mostly what they yell. Everybody fights about it. Even Jessie's been in some fights. I didn't see her, but I did see another a few months ago. I got so frightened *that* time I did throw up. One of the worst things was what I was thinking about, how, like, at first I was afraid she would get hurt and I started to cry, and then, without even thinking about it, I found myself hoping she would kill this white girl. I was crying but I wanted her to kill the white girl. I think mostly because the girl was white and because of what she said. She called Jessie some horrible name, I didn't even understand it at first. Jessie didn't either, but you could tell it wasn't a compliment.

Then, you know, when they fight, everybody crowds round and then they start fighting, like they did this one time when Jessie fought this girl Shea. They were all fighting, and I ran away because I got scared. That time I told my mother, which I usually don't do. My mother told me she was going to school to see what was happening. She went too, but the master told her there was nothing the school could do if children fought before or after school; it wasn't their responsibility. He didn't think the fighting was all that bad. 'Kids have always fought', that's what he told my mother. He said he was surprised she would find all this new. Didn't she have fights in her neighbourhood where she went to school? That's what he told her. I mean, that's what I know he told her, because some of the other things she wouldn't tell me, but she told my father. I know one of them was that I was supposed to be known as a little bit of a baby, that's what the master said; that just because I was a girl didn't mean I shouldn't have to fight and protect myself. He said he thought coloured people were teaching this to their children. She said she thought he was prejudiced, and he told her our kind are too sensitive about all this stuff. Besides he said, he did a special favour for us letting me into the school when we moved here because he could have said no because the classes were so big. My mother told him no one in this country does any favours for us and he told her she was wrong; that's all coloured people do is ask for favours. Anyway, he said there's nothing that could be done about the fighting. It was happening in the school, sure, maybe once a week too, which is a lie because it happens all the time, but the problem isn't the school, it's the country. So my mother said, 'You mean it's all ***our*** fault', and he said, 'You said it, Mrs Davies, I didn't.'

I was surprised too, because I thought the master was a real nice man. At least ***I*** never saw him do anything bad to anybody. I don't know all that much what the other kids think of him. Jessie hates him because he blamed her that one time for starting the fighting which she didn't. I know, because I was there. But I always thought he liked us. Like, Mrs Brainaird likes us. She's always asking me how I'm doing and if I have problems. I don't talk to her, but maybe I could. You can't tell with some of these people, like, how they're going to be if they have to take a side. I think a lot of the teachers would like to take our side once in a while, but they're afraid what the master or the assistants might say to them. Lots of them aren't much better off than we are, I guess, although they don't talk about it with us. Well that's not completely true, because Mrs Strandy, she told Jessie and this other girl how she was afraid to teach in the school with all the fighting, so she was looking for a new job. They had a long talk about it. Jessie told her maybe she could do something to make it better, but she said, no, she was leaving, even if it meant she wouldn't be able to find another job. She'd rather go on the dole than teach here. That's what she said. Then she told them, it was better before they let all the coloureds in. Can you believe her saying this to Jessie, who's coloured! She didn't even realise what she was saying. She told them, it was better before they let the coloureds in. So Jessie said, 'Well, Mrs Strandy, if you haven't noticed yet, ***we're*** coloured.' So Mrs Strandy said, 'Of course I know you're coloured, but it's not the children I'm talking about it's their parents! It's all your fathers who don't work and don't want to, and all your mothers having all these children. That's what the matter is. It's never the children's fault.' So Jessie just looks at her and says, 'Oh!'

That's all, just oh!

Doesn't my school sound like a wonderful place? Now do you know why I don't like going around there, no matter how much I might learn, which I don't think is all that much. Most of the time all I learn is that a lot of people in my school think I'm a coloured pygmy, but I ought to be learning a little more than that. And another thing, if these people, like the master and Mrs Strandy, have all these feelings about us, I would like to know how they can be allowed to stay in the school, and some of those people have the most important jobs over there, you know. They make the decisions and they have all these ideas. That's all we hear from them: it's the coloureds. Pretty soon, it will get bad for me and I really will be able to throw up before I walk to school, instead of just thinking that I do. Like, right now, telling all of this to you gives me the same feelings I have before I walk there in the morning. It's like I need my lucky black and white cat to tell you what I *think* about school, and we aren't anywhere near school now, are we? I'm not sure where we are here, but it feels that we're a long, long way from school. At least I hope it's a long way from school. I know this isn't really a holiday but I'm trying to pretend it is.

*Polly Davies, interviewed in hospital*

# *Acting it out*

## Writing and performing a play on sexism

*Scene:* an infant school classroom. Children playing with toys, and teacher going round to each of them, encouraging them.

*Teacher:* Come on Paul. Out of the wendy house, you big sissy, and go and play with the cars like the other boys. Now Diane, what a tomboy. Leave the cars alone and go and play with the dolls. That's right, Jill. What's your dolly called? That's a good name. Are you changing her nappy like your mummy does with your baby? Good girl. What a big gun, David. Are you going to be a big strong soldier like your daddy? An engine driver? Yes, good boy. Now, everybody come and sit round me. We're going to do some reading and look at some pictures.

(The teacher reads from the Ladybird reading scheme: these are actual quotes.)

'"I want to be a big man," says Peter. "I don't want to be so big," says Jane.' 'When everything was ready, the girls shouted to the boys, and they came into the kitchen for cakes and jam.'

Now look at these pictures. What's this? Yes, a doctor and a nurse. The doctor will make you better, won't he? And the nurse is helping the doctor, isn't she? She makes his tea, and looks after his patients. Which of you girls would like to be a nurse? My goodness, what a lot! Good. Now, what's this? Yes, a policeman. My goodness, isn't he big and strong. He will always help you, won't he? That's a very important job, isn't it, being a policeman? Now, who's this? Yes, good, Diane. It's a mummy, isn't it, and she's doing the housework. Every day while you're at school your mummies sweep the floor and make the beds and cook the tea, don't they? It's nice to have mummy looking after you and daddy isn't it, while daddy is out to work? How many of you girls want to be mummies? Don't you , Jill? Put your hand up then. Ah, yes I thought so. All the girls. Good. Last one. Yes, a postman. That's a very important job, isn't it? Bringing around the post. Isn't he strong, carrying that big sack.

Now, girls first, line up at the door. Lovely and quiet, weren't they boys? Now it's your turn. Not quite so nicely, but never mind. Out you go.

### *What gets on our nerves about sexism in our school?*

All the usual things, like sitting separately in assembly, and lining up separately for lunch. And football. We get the chance to do it at our school but it's been made really difficult. We turned up for a practice, and there was one ball for 70 girls! Obviously they never thought so many girls would turn up. And the equipment we get is all old stuff – the boys' teams get all the new stuff. Finally we were given somewhere to practise, but even now it's difficult to get the facilities, even though we've got a special teacher. And over the years we've raised loads of money for facilities we don't benefit from. Like the mini-bus, which we reckon we pretty well paid for, but it's nearly always in use by the boys for matches and expeditions. Sometimes if they really try, girls can get into a sailing group or something, but then, when they go in the bus with the boys, they have to sit at the back! Most girls in our school have never been anywhere at all in that bus, which we paid for. Then of course there's the subject options. There's all sorts of subjects we wanted to take, like woodwork and technical drawing, but we were told we'd have to give a good reason. What good reason? The boys didn't have to give a good reason for taking so-called girls' subjects. And even if you go down our physics labs, it's all boys.

*Scene:* secondary school, exam time.

*Student* (reading from recent (real) exam paper): Certificate of Secondary Education. Housecraft Paper 1973. 'Your brother and his friend are arriving home after walking all night on a sponsored walk. Iron his shirt that you have previously washed, and press a pair of his trousers ready for him to change into. Cook and serve a substantial breakfast for them, including toast, and lay the table ready for them. Make your mother and yourself a midday salad . . .'

### *Choosing subject options*

Loads of girls have to do child development. But boys don't – well, only one. We don't learn anything – it's things you know from your common sense – the only difference being you have to write it all down. So you could miss a whole year of it and still pass your exam. It's all what a baby does at five months, what a baby does at ten months. First he moves his little hand, then he moves his little foot. And the books are very sexist, assuming you're all girls, and that you're all naturally going to be mothers. There's never much mention of fathers at all. When you bring a child up, anyway, you do it the way you want, not the way some book tells you. Babies' parties! We had to make little paper hats. And we had to spend time at the nursery school when we wanted to be in school studying for our exams.

Then some of us had to do business studies, because they said we weren't good enough to do English literature. Two boys took it – they didn't realise what it was. They thought it really was the study of business. The typing teacher has a go at all the girls, but the boys sit at the back, going, tap, tap. She's very sympathetic to them. She says, 'Oh come on lads, let me show you!' and she does it for them.

## *Reactions to our play*

Some teachers have liked it, but in general the attitude has been that since we've been in it we're more likely to cause trouble, or alternatively that we have loads of time on our hands to help with other things outside lessons. One teacher accused us of going left-wing. Well – we are. That's a lot better than just sitting back and accepting things. At least we're trying to do something about it. So we told him we were going to do a play about racism. And he said, 'There you are! See! See!'

Some of our friends, even though they think the play is good, still keep the same ideas in their heads. Take the bit about sex education – they think sex is dirty no matter how you talk about it. And they say, 'Why did you go on about periods?' They think that's embarrassing, and they look down at the floor during that scene. Well, I suppose even some of us were embarrassed about talking openly about periods before we worked on this play. But even though we might not have changed their minds, we brought things to the surface, made them conscious. One girl said she'd been a part of these attitudes all her life but she'd never seen them this clearly before.

*Scene:* girl goes around a circle of friends and acquaintances looking for help and advice about her pregnancy.

*Boyfriend:* I know I'm Laura's boyfriend, but I can't take the responsibility for this. She should have told me she wasn't on the pill. Anyway I've got my other girlfriends to think of.

*Girlfriend:* I'm her best friend. But I think she's been really stupid. Why didn't she take precautions?

*Teacher:* Oh dear. Such a nice girl too. I suppose it's her parents' fault. I'll have to tell the head.

*Mother:* Where did I go wrong? And it's going to be such an embarrassment.

*Headmaster:* I can't possibly allow her to come in and take her examinations. It's such a bad example for the first years.

*Next door neighbour:* Hmm, wonder who the father is. I'll have to get to the bottom of this.

### *Streaming*

So far as sexism goes, we were probably the same as all the other girls before we started working on the play. Although we'd noticed sexism, and thought it unfair, it wasn't that which made us angry at first. What really pissed us off, very early on in this school, was streaming. Right from the beginning the teachers started calling us thick. Yes, they tell you outright, to your face. 'Has anyone ever told you you're thick?' Bloody hell! What *is* this? We've been really angry and upset, and this has been going on for five years. And then they have the nerve to write on your report that your trouble is you've no confidence. Well, how the hell could we have confidence? And when we were confident, about the play, they told us off for being big-headed. So it all started with that, with being labelled thick.

Our school has eight streams. When you come here if you're Black, or working class white, or coloured, or Greek or Turkish Cypriots, you automatically get put into the lower streams. Recently a girl of fourth year age came back again to this area from spending some time in Jamaica. The teacher said to one of us who is Black, 'What stream are you in?' On hearing it was stream four, he said, 'Yes, that's the one I was thinking of for her,' and that was it! Sometimes a Black person, or a white working class one, might make it into a higher stream. The other children can't believe it. 'What's that thickie doing in here?' Our new headmaster says he's going to end streaming and we hear people say all the time, 'Thank goodness we're not coming into the new first form. I'd hate to be taught with all the thickies.'

We've had nothing but this sort of thing all the

time – racist comments, thickies, dunces. We reckoned we'd start with a play on sexism, and if we can get that out, maybe it's a start on getting the whole thing out. Sexism, racism, streaming and class – it's all the same system, and it's all got to come out.

*Linda, Dawn, Jasmine, Diane, Cynthia, Lynda.*

# *Oh mah gawd, we've got a right one 'ere!*

I am at a mixed grammar school, and when I first came here, I didn't think it was particularly sexist, as I had come from a very sexist junior school, where girls were taught they should play with dolls, and boys to be Big and Tough (and beat each other up).

So the sexism at my new school didn't seem so blatant, because the boys were allowed to do cookery and needlework, and the girls do woodwork and metalwork. However I soon discovered that sexism gets everywhere. In my first week we had a history lesson in which we were learning about Mohammed and Islam. The (male) teacher asked me if I would like to be a Muslim. I said no, and he asked why. Apart from the fact that I am an atheist and saw no reason to change my religion, I said that I did not agree with purdah and male chauvinism. He said, 'Are you one of those women's libbers, then, girl?' I said yes, to which he replied, 'Oh mah gawd, we've got a right one 'ere.' I thought I must be some sort of crank because everyone, including the other girls, laughed. I only had a vague idea of what 'women's lib' was, but I knew I supported it, because the 'women's libbers' everyone hated were the only people who didn't want to stop me doing things I considered worthwhile just because I was a girl.

There's a history teacher at our school who never stops insulting women. He says we never stop 'gossiping' – he never shuts up himself. Once in a lesson on Nazi Germany he told us how clever Hitler was to stop all married women from working, because it solved unemployment, and that the British Government should do the same thing. Recently he gave us a test, and worked out that the average boy's mark was 1.5 higher than the average girl's. He said this proved that men are superior to women. How stupid can you get?

In an art lesson once the (female) teacher said: 'Today we are going to draw aeroplanes. The ladies (sic) may like to draw birds instead.' I drew an aeroplane. In a geography lesson, the (male) teacher complained about my untidy map, saying, 'I thought girls were supposed to be able to draw neatly.' And there are innumerable examples of teachers making this sort of remark.

At my school the headteacher, the deputy head, and the heads of block are all males. There's a senior mistress, but no senior master, presumably because they think the head will always be a man, anyway. All the senior mistress does is to tell the girls off for wearing the wrong colour blouse or something. Last year, all the fourth year girls had to attend a lecture on the follies of wearing high-heeled shoes. The boys didn't have to go! To make this even more patronising, the lecturer was a man. If this happens again next year (when I'm in the fourth year) we shall try to organise a boycott.

Obviously most text books are sexist. I once went through my school physics book and counted

80 pictures of people doing experiments. Only one of these was a girl, all the rest were male. In the series of French books used at our school from first to fifth year, the girls are always shown staying at home helping their mothers with the housework, while the boys are out fishing, and their fathers are at work. Other text books, and teachers, constantly refer to the human race as 'Man'. If you ask why, they reply that it means women too. Of course it doesn't. Man means men, and has nothing to do with the other half of the human race which is female.

There is a great deal of opposition to feminism among the pupils as well as the staff. The boys just laugh at it, and often make it clear that they don't like us trespassing on male preserves – like the metalwork room. While the girls are afraid of being ridiculed if people think they are 'women's libbers' – they never say feminist.

When I ask people why they are sexist, they always say that people are different, and if we had equality, everyone would be the same. (The usual Tory line.) They don't seem to realise that the individuality of women – and men too – is suppressed by the sexism which flourishes under capitalism. Obviously at an old-fashioned grammar school like mine, you'd expect to find rigid attitudes, but there is sexism in ***every*** school. The way it's drummed into us is indeed what some people actually mean by education. Judging by the attitudes of people my own age, and the way we are being conditioned at school, sexism is definitely alive and kicking, and will survive for a long time to come.

*Jenny Smith*

# *Soft and soppy, eh?*

STUART: I think girls are too soft and soppy. They can't play football because they can't play. All they play is champ and skipping. I don't see why we should let them play. They should play together and mind their own business. If they want to play football they should play it with other girls and leave us alone, because they can't play properly. They should have asked us a long time ago. They sulk if they can't have their own way more than men. When grown women run, their breasts get in the way and it slows them down a bit.

*CARMEL: When the husband is at work most of the time the woman has to look after things. Well, I think that is wrong. Why can't the man stay at home and the lady go to work? I think she'll be quite capable to earn her pay.*

CHRISTOPHER: Men make people, by making love to women. And also women make babies too, but if there wasn't a man there would be no baby. So if the girls join women's lib they will never have a baby.

*JANICE: Boys and girls are the same in lots of ways: they're both human. I don't see why girls can't play football, because we would have the same skills if we knew the rules and had practice. The only reason we don't know how to play is because they won't let us. In Scotland, men wear kilts and trousers, and the only reason boys don't wear skirts is because they'd feel like sissies, they won't be, but they just think that. Boys think that girls are little delicate things, but we're not – I bet if we tried we could lift up a bar weight or punch a punch bag – but it's the men that won't let us.*

CHARLEY: I think girls are very well off and shouldn't come and bother us to play our games. They are always complaining about how they need new dresses and shoes. But men don't – they just take their wallet and go. I'm happy to be a boy because they're tough and can defend themselves, but girls just stand there and scream.

*HUMAIRA: I would like to be a boy because you can ride a bicycle. I always ask my dad for a bike but he won't give me one. And if you are a man, you can get a job more quickly.*

PAUL: I wouldn't like to be a girl because I wouldn't be able to go to the toilet properly. And I wouldn't be so strong because girls are very very weak, and I wouldn't play sissy games like ring-a-ring-a-roses, and I wouldn't like to have long finger nails.

*EMMA: For some wives it's horrid because if they don't go to work they have to clean the clothes, wash up, clean the house, make breakfast, lunch and tea. Later on some fathers come home from work and say, 'Make me some tea please.' Carmel says she wants to be a policewoman. Stuart says policewomen only make the coffee, but Mrs McGlyn says Mrs Carl was a policewoman and she was on the beat all day.*

ANDREW: I'd hate to be a girl because girls always have to keep clean and have to help mummy in the house and are not allowed to climb trees.

*Students at a London primary school*

# *'This book is for boys, and about boys . . .'*

I have recently moved up North and am attending a Middle School. During my time here I have been put out a little by the attitudes of some of the teachers towards the girls. In the games lessons the girls have a choice: rounders, tennis and sometimes volley ball in the summer, and in the winter hockey and netball. But the boys have a much more varied choice: rounders, tennis, soft-ball, volley ball and cricket in the summer, and rugby or football in the winter. A lot of the girls fancy cricket and football, and even rugby. The boys laugh at us – it's not surprising really. They would win in a game because no one will teach us. My friend and I decided to ask our games master if we could learn. I saw him in the dinner line, and I asked him about the girls playing football etc. He gave a surprising answer. 'Have you been listening to the radio?' 'No', I said. 'Well, as long as I'm running the games around here, the girls won't do any of the boys' games.' He then walked off. It's impossible to say anything to our headmaster, as he's a male chauvinist pig as well.

But even if we cannot play football we are expected to read about it. When we were given our class reading book, the class went in uproar – the girls did anyway. The book was called ***The Goalkeeper's Revenge***, and when sifting through it, I saw a paragraph saying, 'This book is for boys, about boys. Rugby, fighting, trolley driving and football.' That is typical of my school's opinion on girls – we are classed second, while the boys must have what suits them.

Although there are mixed classes for needlework, cookery and woodwork, the work we do is different. In needlework, the girls have to make aprons, and the boys make ties or cravats. This is stupid, because both boys and girls need aprons for cookery. So when we asked the teacher the reason for this, she replied, 'The girls are willing to stay in at breaks and finish their aprons, while the boys would like to go out and play football.'

I would like the opportunity next year to do all subjects which I am interested in, but which I am barred from at present. Instead I am being guided towards girl subjects which usually end up in family care and child care. I know there is a recognisable movement against all these things which degrade us and exclude us. Soon something's going to happen to make it right for us, but it may take time.

*Debra Peart*

# *Oxbridge – bores, snobs and breakdowns*

When I was given a place at Somerville College Oxford in 1975 to read classics, I was over the moon. I'd applied there because I thought the ancient buildings and peaceful atmosphere were so lovely. Besides, everyone said Oxford was the best university in the country and the prospect of being taught by the best brains was exciting. But it turned out very different – it was an immense struggle to finish the course and I wish I'd gone to a different university and done a different course.

My first experience was culture shock. I suppose I'm lower middle class; I hadn't met any public school products before and suddenly they were all around me.

I sat in my college bedroom on my own the first two days, hearing posh accents twittering in the corridors about the schools they'd been to. Outside my women-only college, everywhere seemed full of public schoolboys with short hair and flannels. I found one girl from the same background as myself: we were patronised by one girl but dropped when she found that our fur coats were second-hand and moth-eaten, not £200 efforts like hers.

Not only did I feel out of place, I was embarrassed at the reaction of people I knew when they found out I was at Oxford: some turned oily, others hostile. My parents were proud of me, but couldn't then understand why I disliked Oxford. My brothers all left school with a few CSEs – one boasted about me, the other two felt a bit ashamed in front of their mates.

The second big shock also came in the first week: there were five men to every woman. Although I knew this fact beforehand, experiencing it was unpleasant. Term started with a disco which was just a big pick-up occasion; and from then on, social events invariably included elaborate attempts to avoid unattached men. Part of the attraction of having a boyfriend was that you felt safe enough to enjoy discos and parties. But I felt really angry that you either belonged to someone or were regarded as fair game.

Partly because of this, many students of both sexes came out as gay; but it meant student life was even more difficult for lesbians and bisexuals – I found the predominantly male town gay club was the one of the few comfortable places to go.

The other side of the coin was that life was hard

for men too; they couldn't have women as friends since the other men students assumed (or pretended) that women were for screwing, and men visiting women's colleges were giggled at.

Many students campaigned to open more places to women. At Somerville we campaigned year after year, but it's only now that most colleges have entered the twentieth century and gone mixed (though Somerville hasn't). We had heated discussions on this issue: some feminists argued that it was better for us as women to have women-only colleges. I find women-only groups very supportive but because of Oxford's class bias, women's colleges foster public school competitiveness, not sisterhood.

### *The top of the tree or the pits of despair?*

I was elected a college rep and discovered for myself the extent of student power. I had a polite chat with the Principal once a week; and when the Governing Body met, we were allowed in for three minutes to talk. The Fellows sat in black gowns around an immense table; their eyes would be averted as we spoke; and if they disagreed with us, this minor intrusion into their academic lives would be ignored. Student politics was hamstrung by the college system – 30 separate units with no students' union building. Most students anyway were more interested in getting jobs with merchant banks than in political activity; some ***were*** politically active – simply to lay the foundations of a career in parliament (I wondered occasionally who would be the Margaret Thatcher of my generation).

I was perplexed and angry at our views being ignored until I realized why colleges accepted undergraduates: we were there to pay for the Fellows' research and to be bullied into getting first class degrees – helping to boot the college up the league table of successes.

I'M AFWAID WORKING CLASS PEOPLE HAVE DIFFICULTY FITTING IN HERE
YEAH - THEY PROBABLY CANT BELIEVE THEIR EYES

Pressure from tutors, coupled with other features of Oxford life, lead to many who start a degree never finishing. Familiar faces leave, change universities, have nervous breakdowns and/or commit suicide. Oxford has one of the highest suicide rates in Britain. Many are students – and many do not get reported in the local press. Always keen to publicise its 'successes', Oxford University is extremely reticent about its suicide rate.

In my year at Somerville, six women started the classics course. One left immediately because she found college life so alien and intimidating. The brightest of us was pushed into a nervous breakdown and left in her second year. I left in my third year because I couldn't cope with the conflict between academic pressure and the desire to lead a normal, balanced life. (I returned later because I wanted to be a teacher – and this gave some point to finishing.)

Besides messing me up, it was horrifying to see people I knew being treated like battery hens. Tutors are there for academic problems; they seem unable or unwilling to understand personal problems. Friends, student helplines and sympathetic tutors provided only partial support: Oxford is geared to producing successes, and those who don't make it are the casualties. The justification is the superb education received at Oxford. But I didn't find it the most stimulating intellectual experience ever. Oxford's reputation for academic excellence does not rest on the teaching – many of the dons would fail teacher training – but on the research they do. The best academic feature Oxford had to offer was its outstanding libraries, which stock everything, including the Beano.

I thought a degree course would allow depth of study, but it was more like 'A' levels, most teaching geared to the final exams. Courses are seldom reformed, because of the weight of tradition; and there was no scope for initiative or imagination. You'd just study the books – one 'man' every two weeks . . . The much-praised tutorial system lost its appeal for me when I realised there were few classes – I found this encouragement of individual competition oppressive and wasteful.

The atmosphere of elitism (conscious or unconscious) and the immaturity of the students meant that many local Oxford people disliked them – understandably. It was these very qualities that made me desperate to escape from the crazy illusion of being there; but I had to put up with being classed as a privileged snob like the majority of students. In the end I was lucky enough to meet some ordinary, non-students who accepted me for what I was, so I could feel at home.

All this sounds as though I hated every minute of being a student. But it was Oxford University's particular qualities I disliked. Studying there gave me an insight into a self-absorbed and stupid elite; but being a student gave me so much in other ways. I had the time and energy to do so many things, social, political or otherwise, and to read a lot. When I met people I ***could*** get on with, this was something precious. I could stay up all night talking, or go to crazy parties. I was able to experiment with communal living because you can meet people so easily as a student. We never found the perfect mix of people but it gave me a lot of ideas and a few very good friends.

I felt truly privileged to be a student – I just wish I'd been less naive and done something more relevant in a liberal university or polytechnic.

*Sheila Jacobs*

# *'When you give up let me know'*

## Going to medical school

I went to a grammar school for girls. The policy there was that if you were a good academic you would be encouraged to do well. If not, you were ignored, and would have to sort out your own future.

I was a good 'Arts' student (English, history, etc) but seemingly had *no* flair for physics and chemistry. I still haven't. Consequently at fourteen I was encouraged to give them up. It was considered impossible for anyone at my school, even those 'good' at science, to take all three science subjects at Ordinary Level. But biology was my best subject so I went on with it, and dropped the other two, since no one had any interest in trying to make me improve in them.

I entered the sixth form to do English, ancient history and biology to Advanced Level. At seventeen, in my second sixth form year, I decided that I wanted to study medicine. It wasn't an instant decision – I didn't wake up one morning with a flash of realisation. It just got gradually clearer that that was what I wanted to do.

Nobody at school except me was pleased. I was summoned for an emergency careers interview and asked if I knew that you could ***not*** go to medical school without top grades in 'A' level physics, biology and chemistry, and that if you were a candidate worth your salt, you'd have maths to offer as well. I said that I had found out that there ***were*** medical schools which offered a First MB (a 'premedical' course), in which these three subjects were taught, and from which you could go on to the next stage, the 'preclinical' course, in the usual way.

But why did I want to do it, they all asked. At the time I found it an impossibly difficult question, and still do. To some people, the reasons I expressed may have seemed hopelessly corny, but nevertheless I said I felt that women needed good women doctors to whom they could turn for a non-sexist, supportive attitude to any problem. I didn't want to study for something that would be irrelevant in the future. Later by accident I saw my school 'personal file': it summed me up as 'wanting to opt out of society'.

I applied to five of the medical schools which

offered 'premedical' courses. Four of these gave me a provisional offer based on my 'O' level results, plus the proviso that I get certain grades at 'A' level. The lowest offer was of three C passes. Two did not even require an interview. It certainly was not as impossible as I had been led to believe. Then I asked at school if I could join in 'O' level chemistry lessons. No. So I paid from my Saturday job money for a teacher (who was actually employed at my school) to coach me for the exam, which I took alongside my 'A' levels that summer. However, even that didn't help to persuade them I was serious. As one teacher put it, 'When you give up, let me know.'

Despite, or maybe because of, the general scepticism, I got the 'A' level grades I needed, and the 'O' level chemistry. I then began my 'pre-medical' course – physics, biology and chemistry to 'A' level in one year, virtually from scratch. The provision of this course is particularly important for women, who've usually been taught science either badly (without commitment) or not at all. Some 40% of the students were women, but this was not taken into account, and we were taught in the worst traditional way, with methods that have been shown time and time again to alienate girls and women students. Lectures, for example, continually left out references to women, except for anti-woman jokes, presumably included to amuse the male students. And many of the text books were hopelessly out of date.

In spite of the 'high' proportion of women students, we are all white and middle class – most from expensive private schools, 'well dressed' and conservative. Out of 700 students in the entire school, only two are Black.

That first year (and now too) it felt like being one of a group of specially imported girls at a boys' top private school. The most highly regarded students there are those men who are both academically successful and good rugby players, drinking gallons of beer late at night in the college bar. There are only two women lecturers.

Lectures from the men are full of inaccuracies when it comes to women's bodies. Physiology: 'a small minority of women suffer from premenstrual tension.' 'The menopause is not a serious event – Valium given over a few months normally does the trick.' Anatomy: 'Nothing is as amusing as a hermaphrodite! One of you probably carries the gene for one form of it.' There is constant reference to the fact, presumably central to them, that women 'don't have penises', and that the female is the vestigial (undeveloped) form of the male.

Then in the dissecting room there are the endless jokes about women's bodies (jokes which are not just made about dead bodies – I've heard it's the same in surgery), especially about sizes and shapes of breasts. As for the genitals, on being told to make a sagittal section of the pelvis – which means cutting up through the torso from between the legs – a boy shied away from his specimen, a male, and approached mine, a female. He said he simply couldn't cut through a penis. What about me cutting up the clitoris? Well, that wasn't the same, was it?

I haven't yet started clinical training, which will mean working on the hospital wards. But I know of women who've achieved excellent results in all their exams but who have had 'house-jobs' withheld from them because of 'left-wing views' and 'feminist attitudes'. Being a houseman (sic) is an essential 'on the job' part of training after final exams, but it's nevertheless being made highly privileged by such jobs being very scarce, especially in London hospitals. I've also had friends who've been very good indeed with patients, but have been sent off the ward for wearing trousers.

Last summer I worked as a hospital cleaner. The condescending attitudes of the male doctors, especially the consultants, towards women patients and nurses really depressed me. And it's sad that some of these women seem to expect and even play along with it. Among many of my fellow women students, my 'women's lib' attitudes are seen as strange or irrelevant. One said of me , 'Such a pity, such a waste' – referring to the fact that I don't see going out with men as an important part of my life, and perhaps predicting that I won't do well professionally unless I keep my views to myself. And of course the general assumption is that we're all heterosexual – it's very difficult for lesbians to come out, because of attitudes and fear of professional reprisals.

There is, too, the assumption that women students will be flattered by the attentions of male students and lecturers. One member of staff demanded that I go out with him over a period of several months. His attitudes towards women were well known – summed up by his statement that he'd personally tar and feather any suffragette he saw chained to the railings.

I'm now half way through the six year course – and still no intention of giving up. It hasn't been easy on any level. The work is hard, the competition fierce. But perhaps unlike a lot of women, I've made it at least part way through a system that is designed to keep us out. My life would have been easier as a boy – I would not have been given up for lost as a scientist at thirteen, and I would not have been regarded as completely misguided and unrealistic when I decided to do medicine. Medical school would be more geared to me, more bearable. I'd be less depressed, less angry. But I know it's vital not to get discouraged, and to go on doing what I really want, and to confront the oppression that we face here. There may be only a few of us on the course who feel the same, but we can support each other, and across the country there are many more. I want to do it. I think I can.

*Mairi Todd*

# AT HOME

## *Young, broke and stuck at home*

In my family it's mainly dad who enforces the rules. He always wants to know where I'm going, who with, and what time I'll be home. If I'm late, especially if I've been to a concert, he wants to know if there's been any trouble. He's less worried if he knows I'm going to be with boys, because then he thinks I'll be protected. In fact, there's usually more trouble when we've been with boys than when we've been on our own.

During the week I have to be home by 10.30, which I think is reasonable. At weekends they don't mind too much, so long as I give them a rough idea of what time I'll be back. Some of my friends have to put up with much stricter rules. My best friend Julie's parents stop her going out if she's been late back – even if she's got tickets for something. And a lot of my friends aren't allowed out on Sunday nights at all, which is quite a restriction since none of us can really go out a lot in the week, because of homework, especially now we've got exams.

My dad's a teacher. I hate school and can't wait to get out of it, but this isn't a source of trouble between us. I've got a job fixed up for when I leave next term – if I was going on the dole, it might be more difficult between us. I've hated school since the third year, when they started to say that if you don't get 'O' levels you won't get a job, you'll be nothing. I don't think 'O' levels count that much. It's mainly learning parrot fashion to show what a good memory you've got. I don't need them. I'm learning hairdressing. But I'm taking them anyway, so I can say to my teachers, 'See, I can do it!' I'll probably fail them all . . .

Like most young women living at home, I can't really talk about my ideas, or what I really feel, to my parents. It's difficult to have privacy at home. No one ever knocks before they come into my room, and often I have to share it with my brother's girlfriend – it's just expected of me. If I say no, I feel mean towards her. I feel my parents are being nosey, even though they probably are not – so I don't talk to them about boys, or bring any back. Also I haven't talked all that much about what I think about racism and sexism. My dad is against the National Front, but he doesn't really take sexism seriously. There are lots of examples of it in my house. Even though my mum does a full-time job, and nearly all the housework, she's not allowed a cheque book of her own. And my older brother makes stupid remarks about his girlfriend all the time, often just to irritate me. When my dad knew I was writing this, he said, 'Tell them don't forget men's rights.' So I don't talk about these things, because they only get at me.

I didn't learn about racism or sexism at home or at school. Even though my school is mixed, none of the teachers have ever mentioned women's issues in any serious way. And even though it has many Black students, and even a few Black teachers, racism as such has never been discussed. Nor did anyone in my house ever mention it. I grew up thinking Black people were all criminals – because that's all you ever hear and read about. I didn't feel I was either right or left wing – I'd never thought about it.

It was through the Tom Robinson Band that I got interested in these ideas. I really liked their first hit single, 'Motorway', went to their concerts, and started reading their bulletins, which gave news about the group, explaining about racism and sexism. I went to a lot of Rock Against Racism gigs. Then in one bulletin it said you should read ***Spare Rib***, and I started to get interested in sexism too. Now I go to Rock Against Sexism gigs too. The bands I still like best though are bands with all men in them. I've always liked the Clash – I'm still punk. They of all bands sum up best what I personally feel about being working class – that we're not inferior, and that people with money don't know it all.

Young women like me don't have much money. What I do get I spend first on concerts, then on records. My parents give me money for clothes, and I have a Saturday hairdressing job, so I'm better off than many. That's another reason I hate school – all those rules and uniform, when I could be out at work, earning. I know I won't get much at first, and I'll still have to live at home as it's so badly paid, but it'll be a start.

I haven't really got any close friends, only Julie. We're really close at school, too, and share all our interests, especially music. It's with her that I discuss my ideas. We tried to start a young women's group at school, but they weren't interested. We'll always be good friends, I think, even when we leave school. My parents like her, she knows them well. So that's someone I can have at home and feel relaxed about. My parents, especially my mum, go on a lot about me getting married and having babies. At the moment I don't ever want to get married, but maybe my views will change as I get older.

*Jan Phillips*

# *The pandemonium*

My name is Vinodini. I originally come from Africa and am Asian by descent. Now I am living in the heart of the East End of London.

The people living in our area are all strictly racialists. This had become clear to us after the occurrence of several incidents like the odd brick through the window, which more or less reflected the resentment they felt towards us, especially as we were the first Asian family to move into that particular closed community.

When I first came to this country, I mistakenly took everything as being proper, that is, totally free from any segregation between people of different cultures.

Only recently have I been jogged, full swing, into accepting a more realistic picture of the exact nature of racialism. I feel I have finally become more aware and cautious about my personal safety. At times it becomes impossible

nodini Patel

to think coherently. Do other Asian and Black sisters feel the same way, and how do they cope? Too many women are still blocking out a part of their life which directly concerns them.

Here is an experience which I would like to share with all my sisters who are daily having to battle with similar circumstances.

On frequent occasions, I sit down stiffly on my bed and wonder. From time to time I despair because I'm uncertain of what I want to do. Tonight though, my nerves are not so frayed. I was feeling bone-weary from over-work and fatigue. Slowly I fell into a deep slumber. I was too tired even to take any notice of the howling and yelling going on outside.

This evening was no different from any other night. The same old kids, vandalising like some lunatics. If I had any power over them, I'd send the whole lot of them for psychiatric treatment. It seems very odd to me that none of their parents makes an appearance after nightfall while their children are roaming the streets and behaving inhumanely.

It is the acceptable norm round my way, that parents do not interfere with what their kids are up to. Their parents only intervene when the 'fuzz' is on to them.

Crash. There goes another empty milk bottle. Don't those kids ever go to sleep? Funnily enough they are always burning with energy and vitality from six in the morning to twelve at night. Every time I hear breaking glass or any sudden noises, I jump out of my skin. From past experiences, I expect any minute for a brick to come flying through the windows. I often wake up with nightmares, sweat running down my face and each time I ask myself, 'What am I to do with myself?' The answer is a dark void.

Suddenly I was really awakened by the sound

of breaking glass, followed by whispers and footsteps as though someone was in a great rush to get the hell out of here. I rolled over so that I could make out what was happening outside. Strangely I sensed a brief unnatural peacefulness enveloping me. I have often craved for a little tranquillity; that didn't mean that my wishes were granted.

'Number 16' someone was yelling from down below with an urgent note. The balcony door was unbolted and then I could hear my dad answering.

'Number 16, Mr Patel! Someone has broken your car windows! Call the police!'

There was a momentary silence. Soon after, my dad phoned the police.

In ten minutes my dad had made three phone calls and at last they acknowledged his distressed voice.

Finally they paid heed and said that someone would be round to do something about our complaint.

This little exchange of words hit me with a pang. I was feeling nauseated, and, by then, wide awake. Kids had tried another attack on us. None of my family knew what to do under the circumstances. My first impulse was to run, run somewhere, anywhere. Any form of rational thought was beyond me. I remained in bed with a sick gut feeling. I was angry, disgusted and hurt by the situation. I had calmed down a degree or two.

Then I walked up to my balcony so that I could get a better picture of the scene outside. Astonishingly enough, quite a crowd had gathered round, unlike the times before when my window had been broken. The atmosphere was tense. I could just make out a large hole in the rear window of the car and glass shattered everywhere.

It was quite interesting though the way the people were talking. Some spoke up strongly as to who may have done it, but generally their attitude was that children always gathered around there (in other words, not their children). Somehow, I had an uneasy feeling that some of the parents had a fair idea of who might have done it, but they were defending the kids by saying that it could be any of them; that there were always boys and girls here from other nearby areas. I knew the possibilities were remote. There is no great attraction for teenagers in our area.

The policeman's attitude was most unsatisfactory. Sure he was the law, but that didn't mean he was going to solve our problem, that is to say, racist attacks. Naturally there was quite a heated argument amongst the crowd even after the policeman had left. Ironically only one policeman had come.

What had been accomplished? I returned to my room with this nagging question. I began walking around my room in a frenzy. 'Why today of all days. Oh, why today. I have got my 'A' level exam tomorrow. But what does it matter now?' I was muttering to myself. Then I broke down into a flood of tears.

*Vinodini Patel*

# *Down the plughole*

I began to wonder after the first day or two how and why I came to be standing with my elbows immersed in last night's soup, battling with the debris of human living and the knowledge that despite my often loudly expressed feminism I had managed to accept, totally, the traditional feminine role of cleaner, washer-upper and home-maker.

The practical reason behind how I got myself standing at the sink was that we have been a single parent family for seven years, living with my mother. When she had to go into hospital, it was 'inconvenient' for my father to step into her shoes. So my brother, sister and I were left to cope on our own, promising not to argue, promising to put all our hands into the sink and to prove to the neighbours once and for all that even in times of stress, single parent families are a success, and that we could cope without that traditional mainstay of the family – the mother.

For me, our middle class brand of single parent family has meant that our mother has become a fuller person with interests and a personality outside the family, and that my brother, sister and I have a greater degree of freedom than we would have done if my father had been at home. Because we have achieved this freedom earlier, we also have a greater sense of responsibility towards, and maturity in, our relationships with our mother.

In fact, I was looking forward to showing myself and everyone else that we could cope as well if not better than when my mother was at home. I thought it would be easy, and because I wanted to be perfect, set myself unrealistic standards of tidiness that my mother had abandoned long ago. She had realised that it was both impractical and impossible to try and be perfect at home and work. Since work was more satisfying, it came first. But I was determined to be perfect and show everyone what fantastic children we were!

But the glamour of living on our own soon wore off and I discovered with a rude shock how lazy my brother and sister are and how dictatorial I become with a dishcloth in my hand. My irritation at their laziness and unwillingness to leap to attention when I pointed at the washing up bowl was increased by the fact that if I had not been trying to be more than perfect I would have sat back and enjoyed having no parent in the house. Instead I made myself the authoritarian. The choice became between me whining, nagging and arguing with my brother and sister to get things done in the way that I wanted them to be done, ***when*** I wanted them done, or doing them myself, muttering under my breath about the role of women and how it should not include the assumption that we are always responsible for the cleaning up.

I began to despise myself for completely giving in to the demands of the sink. Yet there was something within me that could not bear the sight of mess, which conflicted with and beat the human being who told me to scream at the thought of yet more washing up! I became increasingly frustrated and increasingly determined that I was not going to get stuck forever with the washing up gloves on. I longed to go and sympathise with my mother about the horrors of dirty dishes. More strongly, I longed to hand back the washing up gloves:

here is your role, here is your label, I do not want it, not even part-time.

I suppose my brother and sister could have shared my desire for perfection and I could have shared their laziness, but I was the one who felt the responsibility towards maintaining 'the home'. So it seems inevitable that my principles collapse in the kitchen because of my feeling that if I do not do it, it will not get done. So I, like millions of others, will be stuck in front of the sink battling with dirt and a consciousness that cannot find a compromise between a desire to sit back and the assumption that women do ***not*** sit back amongst mess. They clean up before they sit down!

***Kate Ogborn***

# *A day in the life . . .*

## Ruth lives with her Orthodox (strictly religious) Jewish parents in Manchester.

'Blessed art thou, o Lord our God, king of the universe, who hast not made me a woman.'

That is the prayer a Jewish man says when he rises, and that is the first prayer I hear when I attend synagogue on Saturday mornings. I attend always with the same feelings of familiarity, scorn, mockery and guilt. Guilt is the main reason I go, as I live at home and my family are extremely devout Jews who see religion as a complete obedience to the prescribed laws. They would never default from these 635 laws, not even secretly.

On Saturday I put on suitably modest and respectable clothes without even a hint of unconventionality, and on my way to synagogue meet other similarly attired girls. We all smile benignly and wish each other a 'good Sabbath'.

In the synagogue I usually sit on my own, and although I join in some of the prayers I spend most of my time in some sort of fantasy world, dreaming of what I would do if I weren't there, of what I will do in the future, and of how all oppressed women in racial minorities will rise and unite!

Cooking is forbidden on the Sabbath so all the food is prepared in advance, which is an advantage in that women can sit down with the rest of the family. The rest of the week it is customary for the women to wait upon the men and then sit down and eat what is left.

We all say a short prayer and then sit down to a lengthy heavy meal, with my father in the most comfortable seat. We all have to sit quietly for half an hour while he goes through the laws relating to conduct on the Sabbath. For twenty years the ritual has been the same and so I'm now able to sit at the table and look interested without hearing a word of what is said. Communal singing follows, but the women are excluded from this – they are not allowed to sing in front of men because a woman's voice might 'turn a man on'. The serving of the meal is entirely done by women, as is the clearing up afterwards. The men sit back and have coffee brought to them.

Due to the heavy meal and the lack of anything else to do, on Saturday afternoon I usually go to bed for a sleep as this helps while away the hours. Not only in my house but in all the surrounding ones in the ghetto, a deathly feeling of torpor reigns.

As the average Orthodox family in the ghetto has at least five children (birth control is strictly forbidden, except on health grounds), provision is made for suitably supervised activities to take place on Saturday afternoon. The girls and boys from four upwards attend separate youth clubs. Dancing, singing and games last for one hour and then the children are despatched home to their parents.

By five in the afternoon, satiated with food and sleep, I begin to feel waves of claustrophobia and terrible boredom passing through me. The strictness of the Sabbath laws limit one's choice of activities severely. The alternatives are visiting friends (girls), going for walks, or studying the books of the sages. Reading contemporary literature is outlawed because of its subversive effects. In my house and in most of the neighbours' there is no television or newspapers because of the danger of corruption by morally debauched programmes.

I have very few friends acceptable to my family as I have severed most of my childhood friendships with Jewish girls. I have plenty of non-Jewish friends at work, but of course I would never be able to take them home. I do not know any Jewish boys, as my education was in single sex institutions from the age of three to 21. This is not atypical among religious Jews, and for this reason arranged marriages continue to flourish. My heterosexual relationships have always ended in failure, usually because I am very prudish, and would never get undressed in front of anybody. And as I have been reared on the idea that sex is for procreation only, I cannot get used to the idea that it can be done just for pleasure. Pleasure, I have always been told, is synonymous with sin and suitable for animals!

My Saturday night diversions are carried out with extreme trepidation. Driving a car is not allowed, nor is using public transport, or handling money. To avoid distressing my family I have to walk in an area where I am unlikely to be recognised. I usually conceal my money and make sure that I do not have loose coins as they jingle too much.

Once on the bus I am always greatly relieved and feel that I have shed my Saturday persona to become myself, to some extent anyway. When I visit friends they always laugh at my impeccable clothes but I don't bother with explanations – for how can one explain a life full of contradictions?

I'm usually just happy to be out and away from home and family until eleven, when I have to be back to celebrate the ending of the Sabbath and the ushering in of a new week. The oldest single girl in the family holds up a lighted candle as high as she can so that she may find a tall husband . . prayers are recited, frankincense inhaled . . . and I fervently thank god that another Sabbath is over.

*Ruth*

# *It's a boy's life*

## Some home truths about brothers

What's it like for us girls in our families? This is a subject we've all got strong feelings about. The majority of us agree that life at home is far harder for us than for boys.

*I think the mums tend to favour the boys really. They go, 'Oh no, he's got time enough to do all the work when he goes out into the world.' My big brother, he's spoilt rotten. He does nothing. He'll come in and say, 'Make us a cup of tea,' and my mum will get up, make him a cup, wash all his clothes out and iron them that day if he wants to wear them. But if it's me she won't do anything. I have to do it all myself. I dread asking for money, like when I'm going out, because I haven't got a Saturday job now, and when I was working I never asked my mum for anything, not a penny. I bought all my own clothes. I was working in a sweet shop, and I used to bring her home twenty fags a week and tobacco for my dad. But now I'm not working, if I ask them for a pound, she'll go 'No! No!' and really moan. But my little brother – she'll go and buy him a pair of shoes for £16. When I was his age, I was getting those £6.99 things from Timpson's or whatever. He's the only one that's dependent on her now, and I suppose she wants to keep him.*

Parents seem to think a girl should be doing a part-time job as soon as she's old enough. But they want to protect the boys from having to go out to work. If your brother gets a Saturday job then he's great, but it's just expected of a girl.

*Like my brother, right. When I was fourteen, my mum went on and on at me, 'Go out and get a Saturday job.' But four or five weeks later my brother said he wanted to do a paper round, he's fourteen. 'Oh no, Raymond, it's too cold.' In the six week holiday my little brother did a milk round job. He did it for one week and he was the sun, moon and stars. My mum was going, 'Oh, you're such a good lad.' He only did it for one week. I keep on a Saturday job, and I work in the evenings cleaning, and nothing is said to me.*

But it's not just over Saturday jobs that we're expected to do more than boys. All of us have to do far more housework than our brothers. When we come home we have to tidy up the house, wash up and make the beds. Very often we'll have to clear up after our brothers who are never asked to clear up their own mess, never mind helping with the general housework. So while the boys are expected to have either a job ***or*** school, we've got two responsibilities: at home ***and*** at work or school. It's got worse really, because in the old days boys would ***have*** to do things in the house like humping coal, carrying water and other heavy work that isn't there any more, so they don't have to do anything.

*From my sister's point of view, she's out working all day and when she comes in she wants to sit down, but my dad expects her to come in and help cook the dinner. He's for ever running her down. My dad makes my brother do his share, but my brother really moans about it, and went for a month when he didn't have to do anything, so they didn't make him. My younger brother washes up about once a month, and my mum will go, 'Oh, it's really good of you.' But she just says to me, 'You don't do anything,' and I do it all the time.*

Because it's our mothers who have the main responsibility for housework, it's them who mainly nag us into doing it, expecting us daughters to do it in our turn. Perhaps they make us do it without really thinking. They've been forced into the role of cooking and cleaning – and into thinking that we should be brought up to do it, because we're girls. So we've now all been socialised into that role too. We've been getting little toy irons and things like that since we were five years old, little washing machines, dustpans and brushes. But brothers get Action Men. We get things that teach us to do housework, and parents give us dolls, because that's supposed to be the way you bring up girls. We all do a lot of housework because it saves argument and we don't want to have to sit in an untidy, dirty house. But most important we do it because despite everything we think it's wrong for our mothers to do it all.

*I feel really sorry for my mum. She goes to work as a school dinner lady at six in the morning, comes back two hours later, does all the housework, rushes off to do the shopping, and then prepares all our dinners. Goes back to work again, then back at half-past three, and cooks all our meals. She has to work really hard.*

We also feel that boys have far fewer restrictions put on them, like for instance, when they want to go out in the evenings. They are allowed to stay out until any time they like and go where they like, but we're cross-questioned about where we're going and told either that we can't go, or that we must come back at a certain time.

*My brother used to go out to football and not come in until the morning, but if I do that, my mum goes, 'What time do you bloody call this?' My little brother, who's only twelve, does get whacked for it – but if I was just to do it once in my life, stay out late just once, I'd get my head knocked off. Before I was sixteen, I'd never been out, not to one party, never.*

*Then I went to one – and my mum never stopped going on at me. She wants me to stay in all the time. When I'm going to a party, my mum says, 'Watch your drink,' and all this lot, and I say to her, 'What do you think I go to – orgies?'*

We think the reason behind all this is that parents definitely have ideas about what boys and girls should be like. It's bad for girls to smoke, but it doesn't matter for boys. Girls should be pretty, with frilly dresses, and boys should have big bovver boots. When they have visitors, they expect the girl to be the little lady, open the door and say, 'Welcome!' And they think it's not important for us to stay on at school, because we'll only work, preferably as a typist, for a couple of years, then we'll get married and have children.

*My mum and dad say, 'What's so special about you that you've got to stay on at school?' They didn't say that to Harry. When he stayed on at school, not a word was said to him. But my mum says to me, 'You should leave school and get a job.' They think that once you're sixteen you should be working. Because you're staying on at school you have to study – you have to come home from school and work really hard. They think that you do nothing at school.*

We don't feel very optimistic about being able to change anything. As one of us said, when her brother recently got married he just expected his new wife to do all the housework, and our older sisters are already encouraging their daughters to help with the housework. If we have children, we'll make the boys do a fair share of the work. For many of us it would be too difficult to talk about these issues at home. It would lead to too many arguments, or it might mean that our parents would refuse to buy us any more clothes or something like that.

But one useful thing we did think of was trying to write down what we've discussed and get it published. At least other people will read it and see how we feel.

*Angela, Pat, Bernice, Eleanor, Christine, Maureen, Frances, Elizabeth, Lawries, Annette, Louise and Sandra.*

Helen and Emma, at home in Wimbledon, August 1980

Titch and Sylvia, at home in Sudbury, March 1981

# AT WORK

## *Electrical engineer*

'Two years ago I had one 'O' level, in cookery. I hated school and just wanted to get out, but I didn't know what to do. It was my father who suggested this apprenticeship. He and my brothers work in the Dockyard, and they saw it advertised. The careers officer at school wasn't very helpful. She suggested a shop job or a job in a bank. When I told her about this apprenticeship she hadn't even heard that girls could apply.

'My friend applied at the same time as me, and the school tried to talk her into staying on to do more 'O' levels instead. I think boys get given more details about apprenticeships. If I could re-do my time at school I'd learn something. I'd like to do physics; you couldn't do that until the last year and then only if you were in the 'A' stream. We didn't do enough basic arithmetic, like fractions and decimals, we learnt new maths. When I came here I'd forgotten basic arithmetic, and I didn't even know how to wire a plug. I couldn't touch things like that at home because my brother always did them.

'When we started, the boys were always waiting for us to make mistakes. They thought we should be at home helping mum. The majority have changed now. As long as we do our fair share, it's OK. One problem was the way the instructors treated us. They couldn't do enough to help. They helped us more than they helped the boys, pointing out our mistakes more clearly. We don't really need the extra help. They even tried to make the boys be polite to us, stop swearing and things. It made them resent us. Really, it hasn't helped us get on good terms with the boys. There are always some boys who are quick to find out our bad points. They think their male ego is suffering because a girl is doing the same job as them.

'I came second in the Apprentice of the Year Awards (in the Portsmouth Dockyard) last year. Some boys thought it was favouritism. I got pretty upset when they said 'One of you girls had to get it.' I wouldn't like to think that I'm only getting anywhere because I am a girl.

'At first it was easier making friends with the boys than with the girls. I suppose we were competing for the boys' attention. They are fun to work with but you can't have a serious conversation with them. At dinner time the girls get together and talk. I'd like to see more girls here.

'In the first year we had a three month probationary period learning to use hand tools, mostly filing metals. Then we had a six week basic fitting course, learning to construct and read diagrams from a small bell circuit, and a light circuit in series. In the last part of year we learned to draw, strip down and build up starters, motors and armatures (the mechanism that drives motors).

'In the second year we have been divided

into groups of 25 and spend two months in five different shops. There is the machine shop, where you practise simple cutting jobs with different metals. Then shore insulation; bending and handling the conduits, the casing for electrical cables. Then electronics, where you make a radio and a speaker. Then car electronics, where you strip the electrical system of a car and rewire it. Lastly, 'pre-afloat' where you work on a model of a ship needing to be fitted, and do all the jobs which go into that. I'm working on car electronics at the moment. After this year I will be a mate to an electrical fitter in the Dockyard.'

The few women already working in the Dockyard are all in the electrical section, which means doing the work related to telephone engineering, armature winding and electronics. Up until now this is the only area girl apprentices have been brought into. They don't have facilities for teaching boiler-making, sailmaking and painting to girls. One girl has applied for a shipwrights' apprenticeship but Margaret doesn't know if she has been accepted.

Last year a big row blew up because girls weren't allowed to work on the ships. At the time both shop stewards in the union – the EEPU – were boys.

'We tried for weeks and weeks to get something done. We got all the girls from the yard together but nothing came of it so we decided one of us had to be shop steward.'

Margaret was elected. Now the Sex Discrimination Act has been passed, in theory women can't be prevented from working on the ships, but so far, none are, because there are no changing facilities yet. However some of the girl apprentices mean to try.

I asked Margaret if she had been intimidated by the work at any stage. She said there had been no problems at all during the training period, but she definitely felt a bit apprehensive about the next stage – going out on the job.

Overall Margaret felt that though the job, like many jobs, may not always be interesting, she had made a good choice:

'I've got better opportunity, more freedom. If I wasn't here I'd be behind a counter in a shop or in a factory.'

*Margaret Charman,*
*interviewed while on a course to be an electrical fitter at Portsmouth Naval Dockyard.*

# Hairdressing

I liked school but I left because I couldn't stand the thought of doing any more exams after 'O' levels, and anyway I'd already made up my mind that I wanted a more practical skill. At one point I thought about Art School, but you need 'A' levels for that, so as I was interested in fashion I decided to do a Hairdressing and Beauty Therapy course at a nearby Technical College. I also felt like meeting some new people.

It was quite easy to get on to the course, but when the college saw on my school report that I'd done well in cookery they tried to persuade me to go into catering. This made me more determined to do hairdressing, even though it's a three year course and I'm not sure that I'll last out that long. I'll be nineteen by then and I expect that I'll get fed up of not having money of my own. There aren't any grants for these sort of courses so I'm living at home and my parents are supporting me. Luckily they are very pleased that I'm doing the course and were able to pay out the £117 necessary for all my equipment. I'm not sure what happens if your parents can't afford to pay.

At the beginning of the course we had a lot of theory lessons – what hair is made up from, how chemicals affect it and things like that. In the practical lessons we started off practising on a block – a wax model with hair. You can't cut the hair, just play with it! After the first month you start on real people and it's much more fun. It's a cheap way to get a hair-do but clients have to sign a form saying they won't claim compensation if anything goes wrong!

It's true that we are treated in a much more adult way at Tec. You can smoke outside lessons, teachers are called by their first names, but you still have to be in at a certain time and the college is quite strict about your clothes. At my end of term interview I was told off about what I was wearing – my snake skin trousers and leather jacket – but I did really well in my exam and I always change for my practicals. We all wear overalls anyway. I'm not sure why they worry so much over what you look like outside lessons.

One of the main things, though, that I don't like about the course is the way we are taught to make everyone look 'nice'. We're supposed to use hair styles and make-up to enhance a woman's 'natural attributes', so that she looks more like a conventional idea of what is attractive. If a woman with white hair comes along and wants her hair dyed brown, we are told to persuade her to have a blue or pearly grey rinse, as they think that this is less ageing. But to me the most important part of hairdressing is to do what the client wants. I try to spend time looking through catalogues and deciding together what would be the most interesting style to try. Since the arrival of punk fashions I think people are prepared to be a bit more experimental with hair and make-up. It's much more fun for me if clients want pillar-box red stripes, because when you are doing a set it doesn't matter which way you put the curlers in, it always comes out the same.

We don't get the chance to cut men's hair, which is a pity because lots of men are interested in having good hair-cuts nowadays, and I'm sure lots of men would like their nails done or have make-up put on professionally. There's only one man on the course, and when he walked in on the first day everyone assumed he was gay. When I asked why the college didn't allow men to come along as models, I was told, 'We don't want that sort in here.' They're very concerned not to get a 'bad' name – only women are supposed to look after their bodies, and most people here think that it's unmanly for men to do the same. Just about everyone laughs at me when I say what I really think.

I'm very glad that I didn't go straight from school into a salon, because for the first three years you just wash hair, make cups of tea and sweep the floor. I've heard that many salons are reluctant to employ college leavers because they don't expect to do all the menial jobs. Also we're used to working much more slowly, taking more care over each client. I helped out in a salon over Christmas and it was just like a production line. I was paid a pound an hour and I was lucky to get that much. It's going to be hard finding a job when I finish the course and

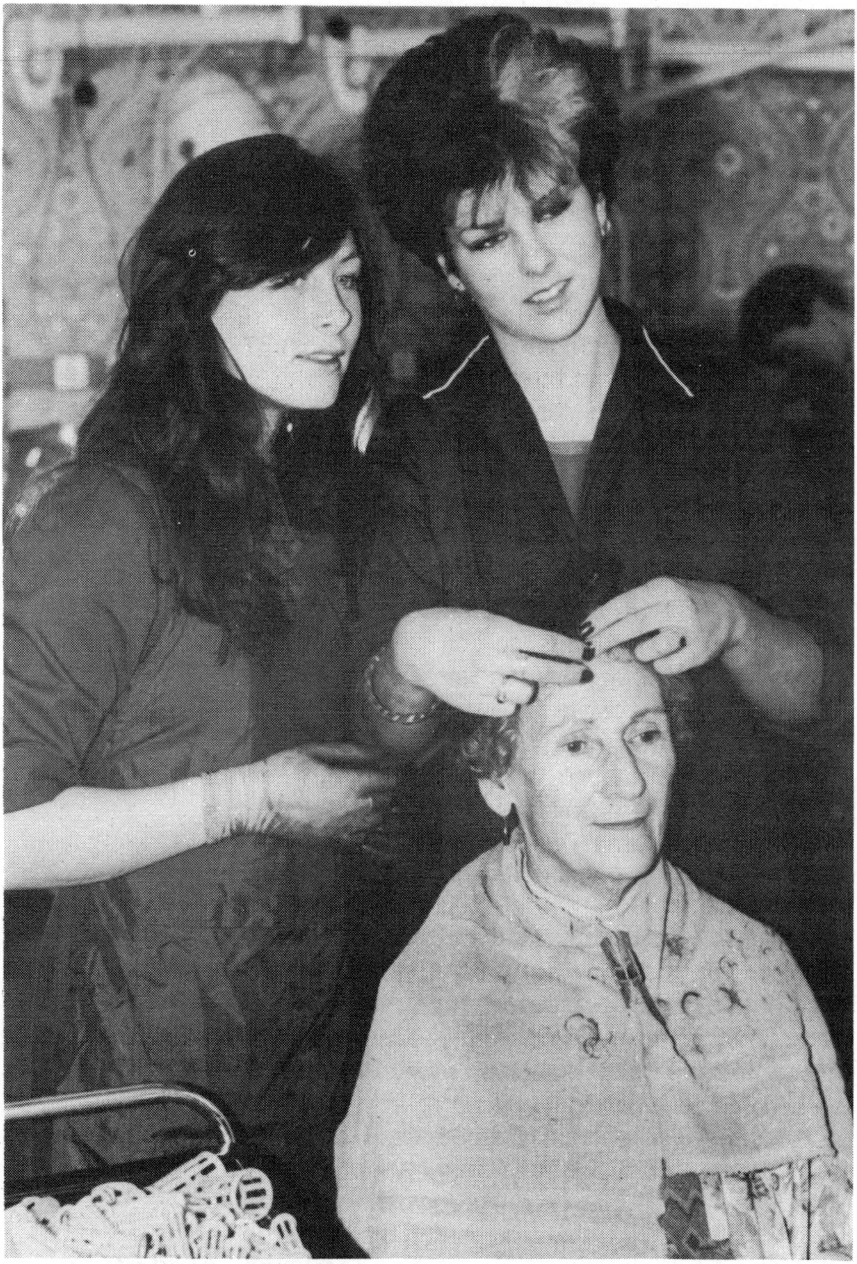

Heather, at college, hairdressing

I'm not looking forward to the future at all.

Ideally I wouldn't choose to work in a conventional salon, but I'll have to get more experience from somewhere. I'd really like to have my own place where both men and women could come for hair cuts, massage and any sort of beauty treatment. My friend Liz and I had the idea of driving round to people's houses and doing their hair in the more relaxing atmosphere of their own home. In a way that's what I'm doing now – I do most of the women who live in my road. There would be a lot of work round here because, like most council estates, it's a long way from the town centre and there are no facilities – only two shops and a pub. Lots of women are house-tied by children and would have to catch a bus to the nearest salon. It would also make hair-dressing much cheaper because you wouldn't have the same overheads.

Most of my friends are interested in my course, mainly because I do their hair for them, but at the same time I've conformed to the expectations of those friends, mainly middle class, who have stayed on at school to do 'A' levels. They think all working class girls either become hairdressers or secretaries. I do hair-dressing because I enjoy it and I don't think it's right that it should have such a low status just because it's not academic, and because it's traditionally women's work. Hairdressing isn't really considered to be a 'profession' by anyone, except for the few people at the top – mostly men – who are seen as 'artistes'.

Often people can't understand why I'm doing a Hairdressing and Beauty Therapy course if I think of myself as a feminist. Sometimes I do feel that I'm not living up to my own standards – I wish I could say that I was studying to be an engineer or something unusual like that, but mostly I try to challenge the traditional image of hairdressing. If you want to take care of your body it's not necessarily for men's benefit, you can do it for yourself. I don't wear make-up or streak my hair to attract boys, I do it because I like experimenting with different ways of looking. It's just like wearing different styles of clothes. I'm not dependent on make-up – lots of times I can't be bothered to put it on, and I couldn't care less if I look less conventionally 'attractive' with green stripes on my face. My dad is always telling me that my hair doesn't look natural, but I don't want it to look natural. I want it to look bleached with black roots.

*Andrea*

# *Babysitting*

### *Late nights, low pay*

Last year when I was sixteen I decided I needed a job for extra money. I thought babysitting would be good, because you are sitting in someone's home, looking after the children. It leaves your day free, you do it in the evening, and I didn't go out much at night. I saw an advertisement in the local newsagent. Three people went, but I got it because I lived the nearest, she liked me, and the children did too.

The mother worked at a taxi rank, and her husband was a taxi driver. She needed someone to do evenings, six until midnight. I had to put the two girls, nine and five, to bed. They were as good as gold until she went out, and then they played me up – they wouldn't go to sleep. They made so much noise the lady downstairs used to come up and have a go at me, even though it wasn't my fault. I don't think the responsibility is fair. I used to worry in case anything happened to one of them. They'd think that it only happened because you weren't keeping an eye on them.

I used to ask their mother what to do about it. She said that she hit them to get them to behave. But it doesn't seem right to hit a strange little girl, and anyway they wouldn't like you and would play you up more in the future.

Although they were supposed to come back at midnight, it was always one-thirty, with no apologies. Just, 'Oh, thanks ever so much,' and that was it. I used to do it twice a week for £2.50 a time. That's £5 for fifteen hours, which is 33p an hour.

In any case, midnight is late enough at my age. My mum got annoyed with me coming back so late – she used to wait up for me. The father used to give me a lift home in his taxi, but that's not the point really.

I stopped doing it because I was getting too tired. I did it Saturdays and Wednesdays – and I had to get up for school on Thursdays. I explained this to her, but she didn't say thanks for what I'd done. Just, 'Fair enough, I'll have to get someone else.' And that was it. *Julie*

### *A good arrangement, and a bad one*

I used to babysit in the daytime, Saturday morning at eight thirty until three in the afternoon. I only had one little girl, and that's my cousin anyway. She was about two at the time.

I could help myself to anything I wanted to eat, and they used to bring me in something at lunch – fish and chips or whatever. After I'd finished babysitting, I used to go shopping with my aunty and stay for dinner in the evening. Rebecca was usually in bed when I got there in the mornings. She used to wake up around nine to nine-thirty and I had to get her dressed. Then after she'd had her breakfast, we used to go out. I'd take her round the park, then we used to go back and she'd have a sleep. So for about an hour and a half my time was my own, really. Then when she got up we just used to play baby records.

It was a good job. I used to get good pay. I think it was 75p an hour which wasn't bad. I used to enjoy it. I liked Rebecca and she liked me. I liked her mum as well.

But other times I've babysat and it's been different. One women wouldn't allow me to touch the coffee or anything at all. There were two very young children. It was ridiculously low pay. I started at eight in the evening and stayed the night, and got £3. I was about twelve then, which is illegal, I might add.

*Erica*

### *Out of control, and a rip off*

I needed some extra money and my Mum told me about someone she knew who wanted a babysitter. I only did it for her once. She had three little boys. As soon as she'd gone out they were really violent. They started taking off their clothes and smashing all their games up. They were just totally out of control. She was in a real rush to go out, and she didn't explain anything to me, just left me with them and I had to put them to bed.

There wasn't a television, and I didn't have

coffee or anything, I just waited for her to come home. And then when she did she got beaten up outside, by a drunk. It was really awful. I had to bandage her up.

She didn't pay me at all, although my Mum had assumed I'd get paid. I didn't mind actually, because she had three children and no one else to look after them. And in any case you can't really say anything, because it's often a friend of your Mum's, or people you know. So you've got a bit of an obligation to them because it's more of a favour than a job.

When you're fifteen or sixteen there aren't many other jobs open to you. So you have to do things by yourself, like car washing or babysitting, which means they can exploit you. It's not the kind of job where there's a minimum wage as it's just something you do now and again. You can't turn round and say to them, 'I want more money in my hand.' It seems a bit rude, seeing as you're in their house, and they've just been out for a nice evening. So generally I think babysitting's a rip-off. *Caroline*

# *Out of school, onto the dole*

### *The last year at school*

– Because our teachers thought we were all leaving anyway, they didn't care about our lessons. We had family care lessons, and also the teachers wanted us to learn typing. Nothing more. They seemed like just a waste of time.

– *I just thought I'd be able to stay on at school – it just didn't enter my head I'd have to leave, and be unemployed. But they said my attendance was too poor. I'd been going to school every day, but not to all my lessons. I'd get my mark, and go out again. I only went to the ones I liked, like English, drama and history, and that's all.*

– I was expecting to stay on too, but I was kicked out. I had a fight on the very last day of term, the first time I'd ever been involved in anything like that. I was holding a bottle, a teacher snatched it from me, it ripped my lip. I called her a silly old cow, let the door go, and it hit her on the back of her head. They said they didn't want that sort of behaviour in the sixth form, so that was it.

– *I didn't really get any careers advice, though you're supposed to in the fifth form. This man from the careers office comes in and you're supposed to talk to him about what you want to do. I didn't have a clue. He gave me this book that had different people doing different jobs – all with smiling faces, and I still had no idea. The school hadn't given me any ideas either. So I left without any thoughts of what I'd do.*

### *When you leave*

– At first you don't want to think about it. You're just glad that school's over – like every year, but better. You know, 'I'm going to have a holiday now.' It just feels like holiday from school. It didn't hit me till I came back from my holiday. Then I went to the careers office. They said they wanted to put me in a factory. I didn't want that, so I didn't go back. I then waited six months, doing nothing really, until I went on the dole. After another six months I got a Youth Opportunity job in a nursery, which was somewhere I'd always wanted to work. But here they made me do all the cleaning, or left me on my own with all the kids, while they went off together for long breaks. Also I had to clean all the toilets. They kept rubbing it in that they were trained and I wasn't. So in the end I left.

I was really put off by that experience, and now I feel I don't know what I really want to do. The careers office don't take a real interest in you if you don't know what to do – just hand you folders, and you have to get on with it.

– ***The first interview is the worst. You're given no help in how to do them at school. You may get a maths or a spelling test, and I didn't expect that. Then, if you don't get the job you get depressed and angry. I felt put off trying again. You feel like throwing something at them. Then, if it keeps happening, you feel like committing suicide.***

– Once you get unemployed, it's easier to give up trying, because it stops you getting disappointed all the time.

### *Passing the time*

– Besides looking for jobs, you read comics, watch television, play records, go looking in shop windows. You can't afford the bus fares to visit your mates if they live out of walking distance. You make yourself useful doing the housework. At first, I used to keep the house absolutely clean and tidy, for something to do.

– *You do anything to occupy your mind. Sometimes my mum gives me money for doing the housework. I have to cook my brother's meals, and if I've been out on a course or something, he has a go at me when it's not ready.*

– For money, I've got a boyfriend who will pay when we go out. But that means I've got to be nice to him.

– *I just go to my mum, and now I owe her a lot of money. But I wouldn't go on at her for it when I know she doesn't have it. It's not easy to borrow money from people.*

– We can't get money for clothes. Sometimes we get money for cigarettes, but it all adds up. If I've fags and my sister hasn't I give her some, and the same for me. But if my mum was unemployed I'd be completely stuck.

### *Your family and friends*

– People ask what you do and you say nothing and they say never mind and that's the end of the subject – nothing more to talk about. You might lie because you're embarrassed about it to try to cover up, and make excuses if they ask more.

– *They look down on you as if you're a layabout, especially if they're working. You feel you're the only one because all your friends seem to have jobs. You get very lonely, and you have no topic of conversation. My boyfriend says, 'Why don't you get a job, at least you'd have something to talk about.'*

– At home it's really depressing. You tend to

get moody and unsociable. You lose confidence in yourself so that when you do get an interview you don't expect to get the job. At first you feel angry but after a while you lose interest. People keep telling me to get married and have children but there's no point in that. You're really tied down then and you still have to go out to work.

– ***Often your parents think it's easy to get a job, but it's not. You can go out virtually all day, tramping around, killing yourself, going for interviews and getting turned down. And all your parents say is, 'Oh, never mind, at least you've had an interview.' They're pushing you out all the time. My brother says to me, 'Why haven't you got a job? I've got one.' But there's many more jobs open to boys than to girls. Your mother says, 'Never mind, there'll be another,' but you feel like giving up because you're so rejected.***

*On this project**

– It's really helped us to get back on our feet. It was like having the blinkers removed. We saw a lot more things, about ourselves, what's happened to us, and why.

We've had a chance to really think about what we're interested in, and what we can expect from a job. We think now that it's important to try and train for a job, once you've decided what you want to do. Some of us will train for office jobs, or for catering. This project has given us work experience, which we didn't get at all at school.

We have really enjoyed being together, talking through out problems. And it's good being all girls, because you can talk about your feelings, get to know each other better, share things, give each other support. There should be more projects like this.

Our main advice to young women still at school is – stay on at school to get some exam passes, then go to further education college for study or training. Avoid becoming unemployed if you can.

*Fatima Meah, Abigail Macnamara, Denise Cunningham, Jackie Jeeves, *who were on a special project for young unemployed women in Camden, North London.*

# Shop work Saturdays

### British Home Stores

I got a Saturday job at British Home Stores. I just went into the shop and asked if they needed anyone. I worked from eight-thirty to six. You got one hour for lunch and a quarter hour break in the morning and afternoon, for which I got paid £7.20. I worked there for six months, while I was at college, doing a hairdressing course. Most of the other girls on my course had to do evening work or Saturday jobs, because none of us got grants. It meant that I only had Sunday free.

I usually worked for two hours or more on the till, then I'd swop and tidy the shelves, then back on the till again. It was mostly girls working there. Some boys worked on the tills too, but they mostly did the heavier work: carrying boxes. They didn't think the girls could handle that. I always used to make mistakes on the till, especially at Christmas, when there were so many people and it was so stuffy. It was such boring work and so hot and busy that you lost concentration. Any mistakes had to be put right by the supervisor. They got annoyed if you had more than four a day. The supervisors watched you, to check you weren't nicking anything or giving your friends things cheap.

They were very strict about lateness. One day I didn't go in. I rang up to tell them, but one of the staff saw me out in the evening and reported me, and I was sent a written complaint. The manager called me up to his office in my tea break. The supervisor stood there and said I'd been 'seen in the town' and tried to make me feel guilty, saying I'd let the other staff and my section down. I thought it was dreadful to do that.

The floor manager used to strut around the shop in his double-breasted suit. It was always, 'Miss Sharman do this', 'Miss Sharman do that', no please or thank you. You had to be on your best behaviour, as the section supervisor watched you all the time too. If you were rude to a customer you'd be up in the manager's office and the customer was always right.

You had to wear a uniform and tights, and if you were allergic, then tough. They had to be 'skin' colour. I wore white tights once, and they told me never to wear them again. One day I went in without any tights, but they sent me out in my lunch break to buy some.

One time we had a load of jackets stolen. Someone must have just walked straight out with them. For the rest of the day the supervisors were watching everyone. They tried to make you feel guilty. Once the store got three letters of complaint, and the supervisor came to tell us off in the tea break. One of the girls laughed, so he started shouting, saying if she didn't take her job seriously, she should collect her wages.

Every night as we were leaving, the supervisors would do spot checks and look in your bag and they always used to pick on me, for some reason. I would never work there full-time. It put me off for life. ***Karen***

### *Shoe shop*

I work in a shoe shop on Saturdays. My sister's friend used to work there, and when she left she asked me if I wanted the job. I took it because I got bored at home. Most of my friends had Saturday jobs, and I couldn't afford to go out much, as my family didn't have any extra money to give me. To work at the shop I'm supposed to be fifteen but really I'm fourteen. I just had to lie, but I don't think they cared as they never checked up. The hours are nine to six, with one hour for lunch and two quarter hour breaks. I get paid £6.65 – about 84p an hour.

The manager's really nice, but the trainee manager is always going on about sex. All the other workers are women. During our lunch hour he sits with us, and carries on about all the dirty books he's read and blue films he's seen. He gets on my nerves. We all think he's stupid and ignore his remarks, which he makes just to aggravate us.

The other people I work with are nice, and I get on with them OK. The customers are all right but some can be awkward; you get out about twelve pairs of shoes for someone to try on and then they say they want to see the first pair again, which you've already put away. We're told to be very nice to the customers, but I answer back if they're rude.

It's a rule here that you're not allowed to wear trousers. You can wear them to work in winter, but you have to change when you get there. I wore trousers once; they said you either go home and get a skirt or you can't work. Otherwise they'd make you stay in the stock room all day out of sight. They don't let you sit down even if there aren't any customers. We're not allowed to stand together and talk unless it's a break. The trainee manager comes up to us and moves us all around to different parts of the shop and tells us to look busy.

You can get a reduction on the shoes in your own shop, or a token to take to another shop. All the shops are run by the same firm anyway, I think. It's about £2.50 usually, but the more expensive the shoes the more you get off. So you feel as if you should buy the most expensive ones to make it worth it, but I can't afford them anyway. I'd much rather have the money.

We have a bonus system at the shop. The trainee manager writes up how many shoes you sell, and you get £1.00 if you sell more than ten shoes in a day. Before this new system we used to get more money – 25p for every pair we sold. The wages we get are according to age. The older women get more money, which I don't think is fair, because even though we're supposed to do the same amount of work the Saturday girls end up doing more. We're the ones who have to tidy up at the end of the day, do the hoovering and put away the stock.

In eight weeks time I'm going to be laid off, because after the Christmas rush, sales went down and they haven't gone up again. As I was the last one in, I'm the first one out. I'd like to work in a clothes shop, but usually you have to be older, about sixteen or seventeen. My friend said she could get me a job in a Wimpy Bar, but I don't really want it. She says it's terrible – she's only working there because she really needs the money. Now I'm looking around for another job, but not for the same pay. It's slave labour, isn't it? *Adija*

# *General maid at thirteen*

## An older woman describes her life as a young woman 60 years ago

A little way past Marble Hill and almost opposite St Stephen's Church in Twickenham there was a domestic agency whose window was always full of 'wanted' cards. These were for cooks, 'generals', parlourmaids, housemaids, kitchen maids, butlers, companions, nursemaids and married couples, all to live in. I had often stopped to read these cards, and now I made up my mind to go there and see if they could find me a job. Making myself as respectable-looking as possible in the old mauve astrakhan coat my aunt had given me while I was still at school, a woollen tam-o'-shanter borrowed from my sister Aggie and nice clean shoes, I set off for the agency without telling mum what I had in mind.

Feeling nervous but determined, I approached the building and with no hesitation knocked on the door; but I was in such a hurry to knock that I had not noticed the sign saying 'Please Walk In'. My heart was thumping and butterflies were chasing each other in my tummy, but I went in and sat down on one of the hard chairs which were arranged round the walls. Before long, I heard footsteps nearing the room and a very severe-looking lady put her head round the door and said, 'Will you come this way?' She led me across a passage to another room.

'Good morning. Sit down', said the person sitting behind the desk. With its large blotting pad and wooden inkstand, the desk looked to me just like the one my headmistress used to have.

'What can I do for you?' she asked, not looking quite so severe as the lady who had shown me into the room.

'I'm looking for a job to sleep in,' I replied in little more than a whisper.

Opening a big writing book – which I later learned was called a ledger – she proceeded to ask my name, address and age, writing them down as I told her.

Then she asked me what school I had attended and where I had worked; these, she said, were for her to contact about references. She pulled a box of cards towards her, sorted them over and after some hesitation picked one out. 'There's something here that might suit you', she said, 'I'll telephone the lady and find out.' She did this, and then she looked across the desk at me as I sat there dying to know what had been said, and asked if I would go and see a lady who lived near Richmond Hill and who wanted a general maid to start as soon as possible. She informed me that if I took the situation I should have to pay her a fee of two shillings and sixpence. This was unexpected, but I agreed, thinking it would be worth that to get a job. By the time I left the agency, it was twelve-thirty and my appointment was for two o'clock. I had no dinner, but there was not enough time to go home.

I found the road and the house I wanted quite easily, and with the time I had to spare weighed up the place in which I might be staying. It looked massive. There was a bay window on each side of the front door, more big windows on the first floor and an attic window high up in the roof. My sister had told me that servants slept either in the basement or the attic, and as there was no basement in this house, I realised that if I did get the job I should have to sleep right up there.

Feeling as if I were going to my doom, I walked up to the house, lifted the fancy latch of the front gate, stepped up the tiled pathway and banged twice on the door. I did not have to wait long before the door was opened by a woman with staring blue eyes,

'Yes, what do you want?' she said, eyeing me up and down.

'I'm from the agency and I have to see this lady at two o'clock,' I said, handing her the letter I had been given.

'You should have gone round the side,' she said, 'That's the servants' entrance. But you'd better come this way now. I'll tell madam you're here.' Opening the door wider, she made room for me to step into the red-carpeted hall, where just ahead of me I noticed a grandfather clock with a round pendulum swinging back and forth. The 'Hickory, Dickory, Dock' nursery rhyme went through my mind. I was shown into a room and told to wait there, 'while I tell the mistress you're here'. On each side of the fireplace was a brown leather armchair studded with buttons of the same colour. The sides of the fireplace and the hearth were tiled in green, and I hoped I could make the tiles as shiny as they were at that moment. The fireplace and overmantel were white, and in the middle of the mantelpiece stood a marble clock which, with its pillars, looked like the front of a building. At each end was a small statue. How different this was to our mantelpiece at home, which was always covered with odds and ends. Having taken note of my surroundings, I was just looking at the clock again to check the time when Madam came in, and right then I felt hungry and scared. The interview was not too bad, though. She asked me where I lived, what my dad worked at, how I had done at school, and where she could apply for references. This was Thursday and she wanted me to start on Saturday: she was sure, she said, that my references would be satisfactory. The household consisted of master, mistress, companion, a boy of about four years old named Peter, and the cook.

I accepted gratefully, telling her I had one morning apron and a frock that could be worn in the afternoons. She offered to buy a morning frock and apron, two afternoon aprons and two caps, saying I could pay for them at two shillings and sixpence out of my wages. Maids were usually paid monthly but, like Aggie had done, I asked to be paid weekly, and here my wages were to be seven-and-six a week. I had no alternative but to agree with these terms, since mum could not help me and dad would not, even though he was in a position to do so: most of his money still went to the publican.

It was about four-thirty when I eventually arrived home, wondering what Dad and Mum would say about my sleeping in. Almost as soon as I got in the kitchen door, Mum asked me to pick up my baby brother Harry. 'Nurse him a little while,' she said, 'while I finish getting your father's tea.' This I did very gingerly, scared that I might drop him. Mum was always saying that he was not a very strong baby and while she was to-ing and fro-ing between kitchen and scullery, I blurted out that I had got the job in service and that they wanted me to start on Saturday.

'You'd better tell your father when he comes in,' said Mum. 'It's up to him.'

'Will you start off about it first, Mum?' I asked. 'You know what he is, especially if it's me that wants to do something.'

But it was not too difficult telling him after all. He was in a good mood and seemed pleased with the idea, which made me feel a load had been taken off my mind. After he had gone to the pub we scrounged round all the cupboards and drawers, getting together the things I would need for the Saturday.

I mended an old flannelette nightie that Aggie had left behind, raked my black alpaca frock out of the bedroom cupboard to be washed and ironed for the afternoons, and took off the vest and bloomers I had on, to be washed as well, so that I could wear clean clothes when I went and still have some left to change into.

On the Saturday morning, I took a penny bus ride to Richmond Bridge and walked up the Hill. I arrived at the house earlier than arranged, and this time did the right thing by going in at the tradesman's entrance and knocking at the side door, which was opened by the cook.

'Come in,' she said, 'I'm rather busy now, but I'll show you to your bedroom, then you can come down when you're ready.'

Through the kitchen, the hall, then up the carpeted stairs she led me, passing four doors on the first landing; then up another flight of stairs, which this time were covered with lino.

There were only two doors leading off the second landing. One of these the cook opened and told me this was where I should sleep. The room next door, she added, was locked and full of things belonging to the people who owned the house. The first thing I noticed about my room was the sloping ceiling: the attic, I thought, just as Aggie had told me. I had never had so much space all to myself, and certainly nothing as posh as this.

'This must be a mistake,' I thought. 'Perhaps the boy will have to sleep with me.' It didn't seem right that this big room should be for just one person. I had to stop my gaping at all the grandness when the cook's voice broke into my thoughts with, 'I can't stay, you can come down as soon as you have unpacked'. A small apron, a lacy cap and a pair of celluloid cuffs were on the bed, and so, guessing they were for me to wear, I changed my frock and put them on.

Then I went downstairs. The quiet was a bit frightening, for it seemed strange after the noise and bustle I had been used to. Nearing the kitchen, I heard voices, and on opening the door saw the lady of the house talking to the cook. She introduced me properly to the cook – whose name was Beatrice – showing me round the house and then let me know the work I had to do.

Once a week each room had to be turned out. There was no Hoover for the carpets: tea leaves were saved and sprinkled on them while they were damp, then swept off with a hard broom. The big windows had to be cleaned, fireplaces blackleaded and tiles washed and polished, loads of silver polished – even though some of it was never used – and the boy taken out for two hours every day. Every morning the kitchen range had to be raked out and the fire lit; then it was blackleaded, the fender cleaned with emery cloth and the hearth hearthtoned. Finally, the front step was swept and cleaned and the breakfast laid. All this was before the cook arrived at eight o'clock.

Middle class people certainly had their pound of flesh in those days. Up at six-thirty in the morning, I never got to bed much before ten at night. My time off was Wednesdays from three to nine-thirty, and on one Sunday in every month after the midday dinner. A good fifteen hours a day at the ready all the time.

There may not have been slavery as such in those 'Good Old Days', but for those fourteen year olds who were unlucky enough to become general maids, this was just about one step away from it.

Sleeping alone was very frightening. I felt very lonely and would have given anything to wake up and find my sisters there with me. The smallest noise disturbed me, and I would lie awake for a long time, waiting and wondering. A climax had to come: I was so worked up and frightened when I went to bed, especially as my room was so far up. Then there was the locked room next door – my imagination ran wild about what or who might be in there. A witch? A man being kept prisoner?

One night I was wakened soon after I had finally got to sleep by what sounded like a terrific explosion. Before the echo had faded away. I was out of bed and down the stairs dashed pell-mell into the drawing room without even a thought of knocking and cried out hysterically, 'The Germans are here, they're shooting guns in the road!' The mistress sat me on a chair and told me not to be silly, the war had been over a long time and I should go back to bed. She led me into the kitchen and gave me a cup of coffee from the pot they had finished with. I did not know it then, but coffee was the very worst thing to give anybody for inducing sleep. It took me much longer to get back upstairs than it had done to come down to them, and before getting into bed I knelt down and said my prayers, something I had not done for a long time. Then I got between the sheets and cried myself to sleep.

*M. Brittain*

# FRIENDS AND LOVERS

## *A girl's best friend is . . . a girl's best friend!*

–'It's like this. If you go out with a boy once and say you'll see him again, he gives you a week. If you haven't performed by then, he throws you over. If you have, he still does but he gives your telephone number to all his friends. For weeks on end you get boys phoning up to ask for you and you haven't even heard of them.'

***–'That happened to a girl down our way and she got ever so big-headed, came into school every day saying, "guess who phoned me up last night?" It was a shame, everyone knew why, they all knew what the boys were after.'***

–'It's not fair, it's OK for boys. They can go about with as many girls as they like. They boast to their friends about the girls at school they've had – when it isn't true. But they'll still get girls to go out with them. It seems to make them even more popular, especially if they're good-looking.'

***–'If I had to choose between a boy and my mate, I'd choose her any time. All they're interested in is if you'll give it to them – and when you don't***

*they pack you in. They always pack the girl in, never the other way round.*

*I've been out with four boys in the last six months – none for more than a week. Right now I'm going out with Pete but I don't know how long it will last. Really they're more interested in their mates anyway. I wouldn't give it to him – Pete that is. I don't want to get pregnant and have a kid. I'd rather go about with Maggie any day. If you just go about with a boy, you lose all your friends.'*

–'I'd much rather go about with Alison than with any of the boys. We have a good laugh. One weekend I go to hers for the night, the next she comes to mine. We stay up talking for hours – sometimes all night. And we see each other every day in school. She's cleverer than me, so we're in different classes but we have lunch and break together. Then at night we go to the youth club. We've been on a double-date once or twice, but it's really better just being with girls, you know.'

*Some young women interviewed in Birmingham.*

imeon and Simeon, friends, at the Orchard Club, Slough, March 1981

Jill and her friend, at the Blitz, Holborn, December 198

# *Teenage sexism*

I'm a Sexist adolescent
Boys are all I want, at present
I can hum a soppy song
Male Domination turns me on
Stereotyped into submission
By the sight and sound transmission
Lisping songs by fluffy females
Adverts showing brawny males
Teachers (men) insist on skirts
Pet the arrant little flirts
Only doing what they should
CONFORMITY is always good
Boys must hammer, girls must sew
Into MAN and WIFE they'll grow

I know every female art
How to play the proper part
Make the boys go all protective
All my wiles are SO effective
Can't be happy on my own
NO ONE wants to be alone
Scheme and plan with all my might
Catch a man to hold me tight
Forget I ever had a mind
Docile, happy, deaf and blind
Get a man and share his bed
That's what all my peer-group said
Maybe this is just a stage
Symptomatic of my age
But NO it's not a teenage game
Each generation acts the same.

*Sarah Hook*

# *'Unlawful' sex–*

## The threat of being taken 'into care'

–I'm fifteen and have just been threatened with being taken into care. I went to court last Thursday for shoplifting, and I've also been suspended from school for having two-colour hair. However, throughout my case sex and boys came up all the time. The police made me see a psychiatrist, would you believe, and when they brought my whole file into court about 75% of their case against me was in fact to do with having underage sex. Often when I've stayed out at night my mother has got worried and sent the pigs after me. The police did manage to pick me up a couple of times and threatened to give me a medical to see if I'd been having USI – unlawful sexual intercourse – I didn't even know what they meant at first.

***–Yes, just look at that girl who got a long sentence in a mental hospital for burning some curtains. It wasn't the curtains but the fact she was having underage sex – they said that she was in 'moral danger' but you would never get a fourteen or fifteen year old boy being taken in for the same reasons, unless he was homosexual.***

–It's not that I don't want any help or advice – I do want to try and understand myself – but in court they said I was a psychotic, obsessed with getting into trouble. They don't want to accept that I'm fighting against things that I think are unfair. I don't want to conform for the sake of it, and anyway, who is normal? Police, authorities, courts, schools . . . I'm losing my whole spirit, but that's just what they are aiming at. When I'm sixteen I think that a lot of the pressure will be taken off me because then at least I can't be threatened with 'care and control'.

*–One of the main problems of having a so-called 'age of consent', is that if you're under sixteen doctors can tell your parents that you want contraception, and even refuse to talk to you about it. I know two fifteen year old girls who are pregnant and they wouldn't have been if contraception was easily available and completely confidential for them. Withholding contraception doesn't prevent young people from having sex, but it's the girl who suffers in the end. Often girls who get pregnant before they are sixteen are too scared to tell anyone who the father is, because he could get prosecuted. This way the girl is left to cope on her own.*

–I think that contraception and abortion are the first things to concentrate on. The National Union of School Students should do a lot more organising around these issues, and on sexuality in general. When they have tried in the past, however, they have had very sensational and misleading write-ups in the press. A lot of my teachers support NUSS but whereas they encourage us in private, I think that they are too afraid of losing their jobs to come out and support us openly.

*–The age of consent doesn't stop anyone anyway, and I think that some girls are going to get pushed into sex whether there is a law or not. Magazines like* Jackie *take pages telling you how to make yourself attractive to boys, and then give you the impression that when they take you home in their cars they just expect a good-night peck on the cheek! Of course, it's not like that at all, and you often find yourself in situations that you're not sure how to cope with. At the same time, parents try to protect you from the outside world, bringing you up to*

*believe that you're cheap if you have sex before marriage, and even then you're not supposed to enjoy it. But young people lead a much less sheltered life nowadays. Just look at my parents – my dad was my mum's first boyfriend!*
–It's the taking into care that really affects young women: there is nothing in the Criminal Law Revision Committee's proposed changes to the sex laws which benefits young women in this or any other respect. The only proposal around the age of consent law is to extend an adult man's defence that he thought the young woman in question was over sixteen, but the young woman still runs the same risk of being taken into care, and an underage couple having a relationship are still faced with the same restrictions as before.

*Two young women*

# Love and romance?

It is hardly ever questioned whether or not romantic love really exists. Nearly everybody just assumes it does. A partner is still seen as being of vital importance in a person's life. But this should be questioned: in my view, such love is a powerful link in the chain of patriarchal oppression.

As a working class teenager at a secondary modern school, I went along with my mates in believing in true love and the romantic dream. We avidly read *Jackie* on how to be sexy and pretty, how to get a boyfriend, behave with him, keep him and how, when you fell in love with the right one, it would be for ever (lesbianism was never mentioned). Our world revolved around boys, and life was unthinkable without one – you'd be a failure, not quite a woman. Friends would pity you and arrange blind dates. But most of the lads were revolting. My mother would say, 'Never mind, there's plenty more fish in the sea,' which was no comfort whatsoever.

Although the word love was bandied about carelessly, we all knew precisely what it 'meant': one day we'd meet him, fall in love, and get married. But what a problem, because in reality, you went out with Alec, who could only talk about cars, or John, who was silent, and only wanted snogging sessions. These boys at least paid for us and brought us presents, but if a better one came along, you chucked them. And if they chucked you, you felt it was because you were too spotty, fat, or boring. Or in my case, it was usually because I behaved too clever. You always had to pretend to be thicker than them if you wanted to keep them . . . so slowly I began to realise how impossible the dream of 'Mr Right' was – none of them were gods, they were just as ordinary, weak and stupid as girls were, and I certainly wasn't prepared to pretend to be even more stupid just to please them. It began to seem to me that romantic love was an illusion based on pretending they were something they were not (and pretending you were something else too).

Having done away with the myth of Mr Right, the next step was to question the myth of the perfect marriage. A lot of my mates seemed to see only as far ahead as their white wedding and honeymoon, but I was less starry-eyed. I saw the years ahead that they would spend with their hubbies. I only had to look around to see unappealing examples of what those years could contain. Marriage is hard work, and in the case of my parents, it was my mother who had done most of the readjusting. In any case, my parents and relatives warned me against early marriage: 'Have fun first.' Well, I reasoned, why bother to give up the fun?

By eighteen I had begun to read feminist literature, and as I did so a sense of relief came over me, as these books often, too, questioned marriage. By now I had moved away from my family, unreached by their desire to control my own role in life. Much as I admired my mother, I needed an enforced distance to develop my independence from her. By moving away from my family, and beginning to read about feminist ideas, I began to be able to move on from rejecting love and marriage to rejecting the idea of the family. And as my feeling of self-sufficiency grew, I began to see the whole idea of romantic love, and everything attached to it, as a man-made trap, to trick women into dependence, to curtail their strength as individuals, by channelling it into caring for *them*. A woman is expected to care for her partner (and children) above all else.

Meanwhile friends were falling in love, pathetically whimpering, 'He doesn't love me' or, 'He's wonderful'. None of it struck me as real – it was as if they were acting out parts in a play. I began to think cynically that infatuation was just sexual desire, gift-wrapped. Because women's sexuality is repressed and distorted by society, women are ashamed of their sexual feelings, and can't go to bed with a man without 'loving' him.

I have often discussed these ideas with my

friends, most of whom are with partners. They seem to agree, but add, 'But I'd be very lonely.' It's really amazing how most of us are terrified of being alone. I like it a lot, maybe because I had five sisters, so for me, privacy is valued. I like coming home after being with people all day and just shutting the door. I'm at peace with myself. I can consider how I am feeling, I can plan and think. I feel that women have been selfless for too long – I want to be with myself, or even selfish, if you like. We only live once, so I want to know myself.

I can't stop thinking that most women get trapped by the myth of romance into years of unpaid work, putting themselves last. In a way, I sometimes wish I could have sunk into that safe, comforting myth, but realism kept intruding. To me, it's well worth facing the world 'alone' – sometimes it may seem bleaker, but in the long run I know that I'll be more liberated as a woman, and free.

*Belinda Yates*

# *Confessions of a teenage lesbian*

In retrospect, I've always known I was a dyke, since I was about four – that's when I first remember 'falling in love' with a woman. I kept on falling in love with them from then on. I did get a crush on a boy when I was about ten – except he looked like a girl, and anyway, I was still into various women at the same time. At about twelve, I went to my mother and said, 'Do you think I'm a lesbian?' I was beginning to think it was a bit strange that I never fell in love with boys. My poor mother, who'd been thinking, 'I wonder if she's a lesbian?' said, 'Oh no, of course not, it's very normal at your age, most girls get these kinds of crushes.'

About that time, around twelve and thirteen, when I was busy ignoring any of my own feelings for women, the idea of lesbianism actually made me feel sick. Because what I thought lesbians were was big butch women doing strange things, which didn't have anything to do with what I felt, or with any of the people I was falling in love with.

At fifteen I was having to deal with feelings for one of my women teachers – corny but true. I kept telling myself, 'This is just a crush, I'll grow out of it,' when in fact I didn't think she was 'wonderful' and 'unobtainable' – like a pop star or something – but I felt very attracted to her, almost as an equal (except of course she was much older than me). At the same time I was noticing a couple of girls around the school and thinking, 'What *is* it about them?' One of them was in the fourth year. But – when you're in the fifth year, you don't speak to the years below unless it's to tell them not to do something, so I decided to speak to Melanie, the one who was in my year (but who I'd never spoken to before, since it was such a big comprehensive). We got on straight away. So well that I went to her house that weekend. We went for a walk while I was there, and started talking really easily, as if we'd known each other for years. She was telling me about a friend she had in London, called Fiona, talking a lot about her – she seemed to be really fond of her. Eventually I said, 'Sounds like you really love her.' She didn't bat an eyelid, just said, 'Yeah, I do.' I was struck by how easily I'd come out with the question, and how easily she'd replied. Normally I wouldn't have said anything like that – anything which would give someone a chance to say, 'Ugh, what do you think I am, a lessie?'

The next thing I was going to ask was, 'Do you get a chance to see her often?' but for some reason I paused after, 'Do you . . . ?' Almost instantly she said, 'Go on, why don't you say it?' I was completely confused – I really didn't know what she was getting at. She said, 'What, you mean , do I sleep with her?' 'I wasn't going to ask ***that***!' I was genuinely shocked. 'Oh,' she said. There was a painful silence. 'Do you?' I tried to make it sound casual. 'Yes,' she said, trying to be equally casual. Aha! I thought. ***That's*** what it is about Melanie . . .

The fact that I now knew that Melanie and Fiona were ***lovers*** crystallised a lot of the things that had been churning about in my head, but a lot of the confusion continued. I now knew for sure I was a lesbian, but I still couldn't identify myself with the 'popular' image of lesbians wanting to be like men. I certainly didn't want to be like a man, and neither did Melanie. Maybe I was bisexual . . . and so the confusion continued.

As a result, I did eventually start having a relationship with the girl in the fourth year, Anne. (I figured ***that's*** what it must be about her, too.) That makes it sound dead easy, but in fact it took months of scheming and plotting. However, after the initial euphoria had worn off, I realised that in many ways our problems had only just begun. OK, so we were really into each other, but where could we meet, and how could we meet without people finding out – because obviously no-one must. That hit me very hard – if anyone found out we'd both be in a lot of trouble. I felt locked into some kind of sick joke, and there didn't seem to be a way out. Suddenly I knew what it was like to be 'queer'. Maybe Tom Robinson had a point.

Whenever we did find somewhere to meet, we'd be in terror all the time that we'd be discovered. Once we met at the end of a very dark street, where there were no houses, and we were pretty sure that we wouldn't be seen. What we didn't realise was that we weren't the only ones to think it was a good meeting place. We'd both been there about fifteen minutes when we saw two friends of mine, a boy and a girl, coming up the street from the other end. We just froze. fifth years didn't ***talk*** to fourth years, let alone go up dark alleys with them in the middle of the night, let alone ones of your own sex. How were we going to get out of this one? In the event, we didn't have to, as they stopped a few feet away from us, and because it was so dark, and they were otherwise occupied, they never saw us. I had real trouble trying not to laugh. The whole situation was crazy. Things like that happened all the time.

Meanwhile I'd started talking to another fourth year girl, Sue, who gradually hinted that she thought she might be a lesbian, but was going through all the same confusions that I had done. She wrote to me, saying that talking to me had helped her sort out a lot in her mind, and that she now knew she was a lesbian. I wrote back to her, saying that there was nothing wrong with being a lesbian, in fact it was wonderful (OK, so I was over the top – I was trying to cheer her up) and making it quite clear that I was one too. And then her mother found my letter. And ran waving it in screaming blue fits up to the school. However, I knew nothing about that, and so I was surprised to be called to my housemistress's office. This was right in the middle of my 'O' levels, so I thought that's what it might be about. Wrong. She asked me if I didn't think I was seeing too much of Sue. Again, total confusion reigned: I'd seen her exactly twice out of school, when she'd come round to borrow some records. Did she mean Anne? Shit, what ***did*** she mean? This conversation went on for a few minutes at completely cross purposes, until she finally asked me if I was coming back in the sixth year to do my 'A' levels. She knew I was – what was she getting at? She said she felt it was better if I didn't, and that everyone (who was everyone?) felt that I'd be better off doing them at technical college. This was in mid-June – I couldn't possibly have registered for college then – you have to register in February, she knew that. I said all that, and said I wanted to come back to school anyway, as a lot of my friends were. In that case, she replied, she'd have to write to my mother.

Before she got a chance, I went home and talked to my mother, having found Sue first, and realised what it was all about. I was really pissed off when I found out. So was my mother. I'd already told her I was a dyke (she'd said, 'Oh, I know *that*, dear' – I'd given it such a build-up I think she thought I was going to tell her I was pregnant or something), and I was luckier than most, she was (and still is) totally supportive. She phoned my housemistress, who said they didn't want me back. (I was a 'disruptive influence on the younger girls' blah blah. No one mentioned lesbians.) It seemed easier not to fight it. I didn't feel I'd be exactly welcome if I went back.

I used my extra year to do a secretarial course, and planned to take my 'A' levels the next year, although I never did in the end. It seemed a bit pointless by that time. But at least I wasn't wondering about if I was a lesbian or not any more. In fact, I was the only secretary on my course with a dyke badge.

*Bronwen*

# *Forced to deceive*

My fella and I first met as he was walking by with a few blokes. He had rushed in immediately and asked me out. My first reaction was that I would like to, but I could not. As we chatted, it was inevitable that he would want to know the reason why. We already liked each other a great deal after such a short time, and my reluctance to disclose some facts aroused his curiosity. I explained that it was virtually impossible for me to go out in the evening and that the occasional times I did go out were with the whole family, to visit relatives at their homes where they would sit and chat about the latest scandals or watch television – similar to the environment, activities and uninspiring atmosphere of home. Sometimes I would go down to the coast with the family and many of our relatives. Every activity revolves around relatives. Even holidays are frequently spent with them. Financially, this is fine, for there is no need to exert yourself for hotel bills and so on, but the enjoyment is drastically reduced because you are with familiar faces all the time.

Eventually I did explain my very strict Cypriot family situation to this bloke. Strangely enough it did not bother him, and for eighteen months or so it did not bother me either. We got together and during that time, when he continually reassured me that our love could keep us together, I felt as if nothing could touch me – not even the conventional customs I was obliged to follow once away from him and from school. We did not actually start going out with each other until about six months after we met, and when I realised that I would be able to get out of school early once a week and could see him then. Or if I got out of school early due to a meeting perhaps then I would be with him. It was inevitable that at times I would resort to truancy in order for us to be together.

The great and eternal dilemmas are that he lives a life so very free in contrast to my restricted lifestyle. He has not got a job and therefore has 24 hours to himself when he can do anything that springs to mind, whereas I have to be home by five-thirty at the latest, which is terribly inconvenient and frustrating – having to leave after such a brief time together. It is an awful lot worse for him though, because I go and fill a few hours out of the 24 that he has to kill and leave him lonelier than before . (I did in fact suggest that he go out with other girls if he wanted to but he did not want to and never did.)

It's rare for me to go out in the night-time and I have to be at school in the daytime, which I cannot possibly afford to miss, or else I would be doing extra school work as well as homework at night. And it is vital that I stay on at school in order to satisfy my mind, to learn all the things I still want to gain knowledge about and equally to keep the little freedom I have now.

It has always been a tremendous and over-powering struggle to carry on this relationship. There are things we cannot possibly do, such as walk down a main road – we have to walk down the back streets in case anyone sees us. No matter how much we feel like holding hands or putting our arms around each other, we have to hold ourselves back. Nor can we venture to embrace or kiss when we want to, unless we are at his home and secure. What's more, we have to walk about four or five feet apart, which is absolutely ridiculous!

In addition, by genuine coincidence, my father happened to get a good job on a building site which conveniently surrounds the house my fella is squatting in. And if that doesn't give sufficient discouragement, I cannot think what does! Nevertheless, we did not allow any of this to interfere with our relationship.

Although I have gained much-appreciated knowledge about contraception, sex, pregnancy, childbirth and abortion, I still won't sleep with this man I love so much. The conditioning process I have undergone for seventeen years is effective in some way. Obviously we have frequently come to a point where I shrink back and refrain, wanting to go on, and yet with something telling me I dare not. It's a great emotional wrecking process having to hold yourself back and not lose your virginity. Fortunately he does understand, but understanding is not really enough. Quite recently we were in conflict over this vital aspect of our relationship for the first time. Due to the fact that he is a hippie and does mix with hippie girls and has slept with many of them it is all the more difficult for him to have to settle for an incomplete relationship.

The pressures were increasing all the time and the final straw came when he wanted me to go to a concert with him in the daytime. He was really happy because he thought that we could go – after all, it was in the daytime. He got both angry and upset when I said that I could not get out on the Saturday in order to go . . . it was at this stage of our time together that I felt that perhaps we had best split up.

I have now reached a decision that there is no point in messing up my life and as soon as I am guaranteed a place in a college or a university where I can break away from home happily and be able to return if I ever want to, then I definitely will use some form of contraception and once away from home the relationships I have will be complete.

*Maria*

# *'Protection' racket –*

## looking at the Age of Consent law

–Our society denies young women the right to express their sexuality before the age of sixteen. It's not until you've had sex, or more specifically penetration, that you are considered in sexual terms. I want to see the consent laws abolished for both heterosexuals and homosexuals because if two people want to have sex then no one has the right to say at what age they can. If you believe that people can't give their consent freely in this society, because of power imbalances between men and women and between adults and children, then no-one could do anything.

*–You can't talk about the consent laws in isolation – you can't just look at this law and say that it should be abolished, and not look at all the other laws and oppressions that surround it, and at* all *oppression of young people. For a start, we have got to rethink completely the whole idea of childhood and adulthood. It's true that twelve year olds have less chance of making up their minds than somebody older, but this is because the concept of one or two 'adults' having responsibility for a 'child' works against young people taking control over their own thoughts and actions.*

–It's very important how the abolition of this law actually takes place. If some committee just decided to abolish it, I can imagine that there'd be a huge shock horror in the press and many young people would feel pressurised into having sex with men. But things don't just happen like that: there would be a tremendous amount of discussion if there were moves to abolish the consent laws. That is in fact what is needed. Just changing the law doesn't change people's attitudes or challenge the power structures of our society.

*–Some young people say that the age of consent laws protect young women from rape, but I'm not sure that this is true. Although a young woman who has been raped goes through a less traumatic court process than a woman over sixteen, this is still based on the oppressive adult attitude that young women are not sexual beings. But I wouldn't uphold the rape and consent laws as they stand – they need to be completely reworked so that the burden isn't on the woman to prove she was raped. However, no one would suggest a ban on all heterosexual sex as a way of protecting women from rape.*

–The abolition of this law wouldn't simply be an extension of male sexual territory. At present, young women are denied information about sex, contraception and relationships, and this is based on the misconception that if you don't provide the information, then young people won't 'do it'. Young women should be able to make decisions based on knowledge, not only about heterosexual sex but also about relationships with other women.

*–We can't wait until we have the perfect world, before we abolish the consent laws. If you think that this law protects young women, then you're living in cloud cuckoo land, because the largest number of sexual assaults on young girls occurs in the family, and this law can do nothing to protect them.*

–Although it may be older men and not teenage boys who are prosecuted for having sex with minors, the law is used as a threat against young people. Just to argue for young people's sexual liberation is to challenge the whole way society is constructed.

*–Just because there is no law saying there is a lesbian age of consent, doesn't mean that the existing laws and legislation are not used against young lesbians. The power to take young women into care if the authorities consider that they are in 'moral danger' is used to control and restrict young lesbians as well as heterosexual women. Any young woman under sixteen who is having a lesbian relationship is running a very real risk of being put into care.*

–I strongly believe that all oppressions have got to be fought and it's for those people who are oppressed to lead the fight; it's young women under sixteen and gay men under 21 who must fight against those particular laws. The rest of us must give support and fight alongside. That's why there is an autonomous women's movement, an autonomous gay movement, an autonomous Black movement. The women's movement doesn't attract younger women because it is mainly concerned with older women's issues, and doesn't recognise age as a specific oppression. Take the Campaign against the Corrie (anti-abortion) Bill, although this is by no means an isolated example. At least three quarters of the people involved in the campaigns were young women, but their support was lost because there wasn't enough work done around young women once this particular battle was won. I'd like to see the National Abortion Campaign encouraging young women themselves to take the abortion video into schools and youth clubs. Older women do have access to facilities, funds, skills, and they must make them available to younger women.

*Two young women*

arol and Nicola, at the Tabernacle, Notting Hill Gate, April 1981

Laura and Janet, sisters, South London Rosettes Women's Scooter Club, April 1981

# *Going out with boys*

When you're younger, school and home seem all-important to you. Over the last couple of years, the emphasis of my life has changed, becoming more socially orientated – going out and boyfriends.

I think that most boys and girls are conscious from a very early age of a feeling of separateness between the sexes. Perhaps this feeling has become less strong now, but I still feel that we're programmed in our relationships with boys – we can't talk to them as if they were simply other human beings. You tend to do and say what you think you are supposed to be doing or saying.

I haven't had great reams of experience with boyfriends. Most of my relationships with them so far have been based mainly on physical attraction, and have involved playing various games. It's not 'cool' to seem eager, so they always phone up a lot later than they said they would, and often act strangely towards you in public, especially if their friends are there. Most boys I know feel resentful if you seem more worked out than them, and hate being challenged or criticised. But I have found out that older boys, especially those who've been through sixth form or college, are less uptight and insecure about the image they're projecting.

Now I realise that just fancying a boy isn't necessarily the basis for a more involved relationship. It's depressing to spend time with someone you can't talk to properly. But on the other hand, I wouldn't go out with a boy I didn't fancy, even if I found him really interesting, and I couldn't consciously talk myself into fancying someone. I like the look of someone, and then it depends on luck as to whether I find him interesting.

Part of fancying a boy is knowing he is desirable, that other girls fancy him too. It just goes to show how much everyone worries about what other people think. Getting a boyfriend is bound up with impressing other people. You get status when you're going out with a boy – and girls are made to feel there's something wrong with them if they're not. When all my girl friends go out for an evening together, everyone gets a bit depressed if they don't meet any boys. Somehow they feel it's not very exciting, and only light up when they are flirting and getting the attention of men. But the atmosphere often gets tense when boys ***are*** around, and the situation leads to a lot of competition between the girls.

I find all this upsetting and hate the way that for so many girls their success with boys provides the measure by which they judge their lives. I'm prone to seek flattery, but I'd seek that from anyone, regardless of their sex, and I don't feel I need men in order to enjoy myself. I've got one very good girl friend who I see a lot, and we have a good time whether we stay in together or go out. But she's the only girl I know like that. But I'm not totally unaffected by all these values. I do enjoy having a boyfriend my friends admire, and I am looks-conscious.

I'm not completely sure, though, why I go on putting a lot of energy into my appearance. Some of my friends think it's a waste of time getting dressed up to go to school, but I want girls as well as boys to think I'm attractive, and I think this is connected with a desire to feel accepted and successful. I've noticed that the clothes I wear in the evening when I'm likely to be meeting boys tend to be the ones I feel most sure I look good in. A boy recently accused me and my group of friends of being obsessed with the way we look. I challenged him, and said, 'But you do judge girls by their looks, don't you?' and he had to admit I was right.

There are lots of expectations surrounding sex. I think many girls' expectations of their first sexual encounter is very much determined by films and magazines. We talk about sex at school, and have been worried that blokes wouldn't find us forthcoming enough, and get annoyed. I've never felt frightened of sex though, which is admittedly a lot to do with my upbringing. But there's a fine line between being worried about sex itself, and feeling embarrassed or unsure. The first time I slept with a boy I was very self-conscious, but I think now that it helps if you know the other person quite well when you do it for the first time. Otherwise, it's hard to relax – you keep thinking you want to go to the loo, and feel self-conscious about your body.

Sleeping arrangements always pose a big problem. I wouldn't choose to mix my relationships with my boyfriends with my home life, although I do feel lucky that my mother doesn't mind if they stay the night. But I don't feel that I have my own independent space, and often feel tense about this. For most of my friends though, sex is much more surreptitious, as their parents would go mad if they knew their daughters were sleeping with boyfriends.

At school we all think it's a bit stupid for couples to go out with each other for a very long time. It always seems too cosy, and always ends up with the girls feeling unable to go anywhere without their boyfriends, and losing any sense of independence. Whenever I've gone out with a boy who's wanted to see me all the time, and been really possessive, I've felt claustrophobic and had to finish it. A very good aspect of the relationship I'm in at the moment is that we don't see much of each other, and a lot of my social life still revolves around my friends. You don't have to see someone all the time for it to be good.

At the moment I think we both feel we're open to the idea of having relationships with other people. I didn't plan to try to have a less possessive relationship, but I think it's naive not to accept this as a possibility. I wouldn't expect someone to only want to spend time with and want to be close to me. Sometimes though I find myself reacting in the conventional way – there seems to be a gap between my emotions and what I've thought out in my head. I think we both would be upset if the other one started to get into someone else. But it's the feeling of being replaced that hurts, not so much the fact that your lover has slept with someone else.

I can't really imagine at this stage in my life being able to handle or even want two big relationships of equal importance. Even if I did I know that it's rare being able to find a bloke who'd willingly put up with you having another relationship at the same time. I don't have any friends, either, who think about things in the same way as I do – they all think I'm mad! If I mention that my boyfriend has slept with another girl, they can't understand why I'm not devastated. For the most part, I think falling madly in love is a bit hysterical. Anyway, it doesn't last. I suppose I'm not really looking for that sort of relationship. I think you feel much more whole as a person when there is more than one aspect to your life. If I did feel that way about someone, though, I think it would be a nice experience, and I expect I will, at some stage in my life.

I find it hard to get an over-all view of my life – it's much easier to see a pattern when you're looking back into the past. I suppose my relationships with boys are quite experimental in that they involve an aspect of trial and error. Sex is important in my life, but it's not a huge big deal.

Looking into the future I don't think I'll want to settle down for a long time with just one man. But I've never felt deeply involved with anyone, so perhaps I'll change my mind. I think lots of people marry or settle for one 'life long' sexual relationship because they're afraid of being alone. I feel I'd be quite happy to live by myself or with my friends , but you can never really tell how things will turn out.

*Lisa*

# *Pressure, problems . . .*

## Another discussion about the Age of Consent

–I've had pressure from boys to have sex but when I did, the only thing I was worried about was getting pregnant. I wasn't worried that someone might find out I was underage. He just kept on saying, 'Go on . . .' Looking back, I can see that I was under pressure although I didn't really notice at the time: it just seemed natural.

*–Most people are very aware that the consent laws exist. Once you're sixteen you get all the cracks: 'You're legal now, you can be knocked off.' Also a lot of girls are made to feel that it's daring and anti-establishment to have underage sex; but having this arbitrary age you feel that you must lose your virginity by the time you are sixteen. Yes, lose 'it', as if it is something you have too look after.*

–When you are sixteen it's true that your boyfriend expects to have sex with you. But if you do they call you a slag, and if you don't, then you're tight.

*–I do think though that a lot of the sexual competition between girls as well as the moral judgements stem from boys, because they show off to each other about how many girls they've 'had'. It's acceptable for them to do that, and yet if girls do they're seen as cheap.*

–I've never felt any pressure to have sex.

*–Well you're bloody lucky – I'm eighteen now, and must have been the prime example of someone who did things because everyone else did. I've only recently started to think about things. As far as the age of consent is concerned, I think that we all mature at different rates, and*

*whereas some girls feel confident that they can handle the whole thing before they're sixteen, I certainly couldn't have done.*

–In the long term, we don't want any restrictions on our sexuality, but for the moment perhaps the age of consent laws could work to young women's advantage. She could use it as a safeguard, to fend off pressure to have sex when she doesn't want to. It gives her time to think it over.

*–Actually I think she'd be more likely to say that she was worried about getting pregnant. However, I do think that the law makes older men think twice about hassling you. Often I've been chatted up by men when I've been out with my friends, but as soon as they find out that we're under sixteen, they leave us alone saying, 'Come back in a couple of years.'*

–I don't think it's right to assume that an older man who is having a relationship with a young girl is necessarily dominating her. If they are both happy about it then it's no business of the law, the courts or the parents. It's really unfair if it all gets blown out of proportion and leads to prosecution.

*–Yes, that's true, that it's hard to say to what extent young women are or aren't under pressure, from outside forces such as images in the media as well as from individuals. The whole issue of 'consent' really is quite complicated, and how young is a 'young girl'?*

–Well I suppose someone who has reached puberty; I can't see how, in this society, an eight year old could have an equal and non-exploitative sexual relationship with an adult man.

*–I think that it's much more difficult to cope with sexual advances from older, more self-confident men than from boys of our own age. I know that almost all of us here have had experiences, some of them very disturbing, of sexual pressure from men over 30 say, frequently friends of the*

*family. These men are associated in your mind with parental authority, and after all they represent the group of people who have control and dominate your everyday life. It's strange the way you keep these experiences to yourself as if it's your fault. I do feel, however, that there is a big difference between children and young people exploring their sexuality together, than with older men who are automatically in such a powerful position over someone much younger.*

–Part of the reason I've felt powerless in the past is because sex education is so bad. It's all so biological – there's very little about contraception, abortion is all hushed up, and no one ever mentions pleasure.

*–All the bits they miss out at school, like masturbation or homosexuality you learn from your friends in a sort of sneaky, dirty way. I've talked to my friends about everything except lesbianism, but I remember when I was younger being told to stop kissing my girl friends.*

–I think that it's important for girls to masturbate, even though boys seem to think it's so funny. You never see any proper diagrams of the genitals, and girls know so little about their bodies I didn't even know about the existence of the clitoris until about two years ago.

*–I think that a lot of this ignorance about our bodies stems from the way that men are seen to be the sexually active ones. Traditionally women lie back and don't have to know what's going on. There should be a lot more discussion at school about sexuality, perhaps in single-sex groups, but unless teachers themselves are open-minded it would be a waste of time.*

–Boys know virtually nothing about girls' bodies either – before the relationship I have now, after I'd had sex with boys I always felt used because I'd given them a lot of pleasure . . . he could always say things to me like, 'Faster', but if I'd come out

and said things like that . . . well!
*–One of the big problems is where to go to have sex, even when you are sixteen. But it's not until contraception is easily available whatever your age, that we can have more control over our sex lives. I'm sixteen, but my doctor was really shocked and made me feel very guilty when I asked to go on the pill.*
–Yes, just lowering or abolishing the age of consent won't necessarily give us more sexual freedom or control. I wish we could brainwash everyone and start all over again.

*A young women's group*

# TOGETHER

## *Playing with Perspex*

### A young women's band in Leicester

We thought, why can't we set up our own rock band? We can play instruments, so why not? We didn't really think about it being an unusual thing for girls to do. We've been together for eight months but we are still not particularly good at songs and we lack confidence. The competition is quite something – the boys' started booing and jeering things at our first gig as soon as we walked on stage before we'd played a note, and we were already nervous. What chance did we stand! When we first started, the boys' would come in while we were learning to play and snigger at us. They said we were rubbish before we even started playing. It made us all the more determined.

Sometimes the boys say we've only got where we are because we are girls. Then we wonder if we are a crap group. But if we really were, then obviously people would say rubbish and walk out. But being girls is an advantage. There are so many boys' groups and so much competition between all of them as to who is the best boys' group – they can't do that with us, can they?

You could be a good group to look at, but not play very well. You can throw yourself at the audience as a sex symbol – they expect it of you. It's an advantage, but it shouldn't be. Really, you don't want to look too tarty, but you just want to be girls. We want to dress up, perhaps a bit more than usual, but not overdress. You show you're a girl in what you wear, but you shouldn't have to. You like the whistles because you think it's flattering. It's difficult not to like it. Even though we want to be good because of the music, when you go out there you think, 'What do I look like?' You probably do stand a better chance if you have good looks. But when we play for all women we wear what we want to – it's easy.

When the boys make comments, it does affect us. Yesterday when we were playing we could see these boys looking at us from the front row, just staring and shouting. A guitar string broke, and then a strap, and we thought, 'Oh, that's done it!'

Our parents have mixed reactions. We ask them to buy us instruments, but they think it's a joke, or they say, 'You want something more feminine!' It's dead hard to save for some drums. They won't help us buy them, and even if we do get them there's nowhere to practise – we can't keep them at home. It makes you sick – we can play the instruments, but our parents won't buy them for us and we can't afford to get them.

*Perspex*

ɔcking' – Saturday night at Shades, Manor House, February 1981

# *Such a relief when you find each other –*

## Starting a young women's group at school

Ours is a large mixed comprehensive school with quite a big sixth form. There's been a women's group here for three years, though of course with people leaving and new ones coming into the sixth form, it restarts every year. It originally began when three girls announced in assembly that there would be a meeting to discuss starting a women's group. Quite a few people came, and we discussed what sort of things we'd talk about and take action on. We decided to start off with a few consciousness-raising meetings, closed to boys, to exchange experiences. For example, a Greek girl told us about her problems over wanting to have a boyfriend, and how she was being made unhappy by her family's restrictions. We talked to each other about sexuality in general, and about lesbianism, though no one was a lesbian or said they were. And about menstruation and so on. We also began to talk about the women's movement, its ideas and campaigns. Some of us had known about feminism from an early age, via our mothers. A few of us were already active in political campaigns of some sort. Others were just generally interested. The three girls who'd started it were already connected with the women's movement, through the National Abortion Campaign and so on, and they explained some of the movement's ideas to us. We were all especially active in 1980 campaigning against Corrie's suggested changes in the abortion law which would have made it very difficult for many young women who need abortions.

There were objections to us having closed meetings. This was partly because we had held them in the common room, which is the only room with comfortable chairs, and obviously other students rightly object to being shut out. Even when we held open meetings in the room, we'd still have problems – continual interruptions. But on the other hand, if you don't hold your open meetings somewhere central, no one will come.

This is one of the real problems with school groups – getting somewhere regular and comfortable to meet. Your life is governed by rules, bells, timetables, and generally uncomfortable conditions. In an average comprehensive school, younger students are particularly discriminated against in this way. They are virtually locked out of rooms except for lesson times, and have nowhere to go except crowded, cold, noisy places, or just to wander around. As sixth formers, we are privileged. We've been given a special building and made an elite. We're lucky – but this effectively cuts us off from the rest of the students, and we are sure that there are many girls like us, only a bit younger, who'd like to come to meetings. We may think them too young, too noisy, but we've been trained to underestimate them. They need our support and encouragement. It's not right that they should have to wait, like we have had to, until the sixth form to have the privilege of being together. In any case, since this sixth form is largely white and middle class, it excludes most girls from ever being in such a group.

People sometimes feel hopeless about changing things – after all, you can talk and talk about what's wrong in your school and in society, and yet you are often powerless to do anything about it. So what's the point of a group? Is it just sitting around getting depressed? Well, we think it's still important to share experiences, support each other, find out more about feminism, even if you can't get what you want in your own school. And to try and be in touch with what all girls experience in other schools – even if sexism isn't crushing you so badly in your own.

We've also discussed quite a lot whether teachers should be in the group, and on the whole we think not. However friendly teachers are, however supportive, however similar in their politics, in the end they remain a teacher, and in any discussion they have power over you whether or not they use it. You can never be absolutely sure they won't say things later in the staff room. They also basically have more power than us to push their views, even though these are built on greater experience. We think it's best for women teachers to form their own groups, and for us to have ours, and of course for the groups to meet and work together. But to return to the problem of young students – they often have to have a teacher responsible for fixing a room for them to meet in, and even to stay with them. So feminist teachers have an important role here, to help younger girls get groups together and to support them within the restrictions of the school. Also feminist teachers might come up with more ways of getting younger and older girls together occasionally, if not regularly, as they have much more power than us in that respect.

Another area of common interest between us and feminist teachers is women's studies. We don't all agree as to whether it should be on the timetable as such, though we think women's issues should definitely be discussed in all sorts of lessons from a very early age – not just sex education or the occasional 'disguised' RE lesson. We'd like to see continual courses around feminist ideas, literature, campaigns, history and so on, but not necessarily just in one subject, or leading to exams, and not always just for girls.

We realise we are lucky to have this relative freedom – a fairly relaxed school, with several feminist teachers, and many special sixth form privileges. But basically we are still very restricted – everything to do with our meetings has to be checked out first and even the contents of this article had to go through the headmistress before it could be published. There's really no school with girls and women in it which doesn't need a women's group. When you find each other, it's such a relief.

*Jane, Naomi, Julie, Petra, Kate, Jane, Lucy, Nicole, Rachel*

# *No more chaos . . .*

## At the youth club

Girls' nights started up here last September, and some of us have been coming since the very first night – it's every Friday. Before then we used to come to the club on Tuesdays, when it was mixed, boys and girls. It was chaos, pure chaos. The boys rush around all over the place. They jump over the counter into the kitchen. When you tell them to stop, they say, no, you don't own the club. They push and hit you. They think they own the gym – kicking footballs around all night, you just can't go in there, unless you want to play too, and then they call you a tomboy.

Just after the girls' nights started, the youth

leaders organised a girls' camp. It was a special photography weekend, and we had a great time, cooking what we wanted, eating what we wanted. We went exploring, and found a swamp, which was really scarey, and ran all the way back, two miles. Boys would have pretended not to be scared – it's not their image. We really got to know each other, and made new friends. Before, we'd thought we wouldn't get on well at camp, that we'd get annoyed with each other, but we found we got really close. We all go to different schools, so this camp was a good time for us to mix with new people. Anyway, it was much better than a school camp – with school, you can't do this, you can't do that, it's all out of bounds, and you've got to do school work. In this camp, you learnt things together, and you could just have a good time.

There's a notice up about girls' night, and some of us who joined later, saw it and asked the youth leader, and decided to try it. You can learn lots of things that you want to know – tape recording, filming, swimming, drama, and there'll be brick-laying when the weather gets better, and skills like that. Every week you have a particular activity – we've done ice skating too. But also you can talk to each other in peace – and run around freely. When the boys are here you have to keep dodging. There's much fewer rules on girls' nights.

But the main thing is getting to know other girls, and getting more friendly. You can be peaceful here and take your time. On mixed nights, you have to talk quickly, you can't relax – if you offer each other sweets or chips, everyone grabs. It makes everyone, girls and boys, much more noisy, and the girls are sometimes not nice to each other – they seem more snobby, not wanting to know you. The same girls, when they come here, turn out to become your friends. It's important to have friends outside school because often your friends don't live near you and anyway in mixed schools it's the same problem, you can't get quiet times together, and it's do this, do that all the time.

We like having the chance to do sports without boys around. They are too pushy. Sometimes we enjoy playing with them, but we need to play on our own too.

Some of our friends say, isn't it boring when there's no boys? We say, no, it's better without, but anyway there's Tuesday nights if you want to get to know boys. Then some say, well are there any dishy ones there? That's all they ever think about, but it's strange, because, when you think about it, girls mainly like going around with other girls.

Boys tend to think we are all weaklings – but engineering and other work they think is just for men, doesn't even need the strength that nursing needs. All a man has to do when a woman is having a baby is phone up someone – it's the women who do all the work. At school, boys are always using swearing words. Half of them don't know what they mean, it's just acting tough. Like all these skinhead haircuts, and wearing all these posh things that are in the fashion now . . . but at this Friday club you don't have to bother about any of that, it's relaxed, it's exciting, and every time you come you learn more things. At school it's always, sshh, put your hands up. Like as if you're under command, if you don't do something, you'll be shot. Go and stand outside the door!! And you can't talk there about girls' things. Like if you have your period, you can't say to a man teacher that you want to go out of the room because your period has started. You have to say you want to go to the toilet – and he just won't believe you. But here everyone understands those things. We can talk privately to each other. You can talk to boys too, about these things, they know a lot of things nowadays, but often we'd still just like to talk to girls . . . just ordinary things, like what happened to you today, what troubles you've been in. Girls here always listen. Boys don't listen, they just go, so what! We know boys who do like to be quiet, even ones who like sewing, working with fabrics. But when the other boys come round, they say they don't like it, and then they give it up.

Boys say, when I'm grown up I'm going to get a nice girl who'll cook nice meals. We're slaves when we're young, and we're slaves when we're older. But when we're older we're going to make sure he helps with all the work – there'll be no excuses that he's been out to work all day.

Some people say to us that it's not healthy, not natural to be separated from boys, especially those of us who go to all girls' schools. But it doesn't matter to us, we know that we get more chances to do things when there's no boys around. We could go to the mixed nights – some of us do, but Fridays are special and we're going to go on coming.

***Hayley, Tracey, Julie, Jenny, Deborah, Alison, Ann, Penny, Juliette***

ise and Noelle, International Women's Day, Brighton, March 1981

A self defence class at the East Midlands Asian Girls' Festival, April 1[illegible]

# *Growing angry, growing strong*

Sangeeta: *I get really angry with some of these white people. They have some peculiar ideas about us Asian girls. Either we get totally ignored at school by everyone, treated as though we did not exist, or the teachers think we have all these problems with our parents about arranged marriages, even when we don't.*
Wahida: *Yea, and then there are some racist students who are always picking on us. Recently we had a fight in our school between us and some white girls. We really showed them we were not going to stand for their rubbish.*

Asian girls' experiences at school reflect the general racism prevalent in society. The stereotypes and myths that white society has about Asian girls are found in some white teachers' attitudes towards them, and in the actions of white students either in ignoring them, or throwing racist abuse, or attempting to beat them up. As Jyoti says, racism started from the first day at school when she had someone come to her and ask questions such as:
*Do you live in mud houses in Pakistan?*
*Why do you marry when you are ten?*
*Why do you smell?*
*Why is your hair greasy?*
*Do you eat curry all the time?*

Jyoti said she was surprised to find that English children knew so little about her country: *They do not know anything about other countries. They are plain ignorant. They should try finding out for themselves before asking such stupid questions. They only know what their parents tell them.*

Racism doesn't stop at being asked such questions and at continually being mocked. Very often there are physical fights as well. Davinder's experience is quite common: *When I was in my second year at school and you walked down the corridor, if there were gangs of white girls they would always pick on us and call us 'wogs' and 'Pakis' and everything like that. One day it happened to me, but I could speak up for myself, so it was quite good, you see. I was walking down with my friend, and they started hitting us. They think you are entirely stupid because you are Indian, and won't stick up for yourself. They enjoy it if you don't say anything. I told my tutor about it, told her that they should not be allowed to do things like that, should they, and she said, 'we'll see what we can do about it.' But she did not do or say anything.*

Teachers' unwillingness to intervene in such situations and take action against white students is not the only way in which they expose their *own* racism. Davinder continues with another incident: *A couple of years later, something else happened. Some of the West Indian girls were messing about, having a good time, and the tutor came in, and she started saying, 'You should be respectful to me,' and that, 'You come into this country and are privileged and is this how you use it?' She was really going on like that – 'You come from an uncivilised country and you obviously came here because the education is much better.' We did not like it and we again complained about it. She used to say things like, 'Shut up, you bunch of slags' – and she got away with it. It was that bad at that school all the time. The teachers were really prejudiced.*

White students' ignorance and racism is further reinforced through the curriculum used by the teachers, particularly in subjects like history and geography. Most history classes still teach how the British ruled the 'colonies' as a favour to the supposedly backward, uncivilised people in Africa and India. No reference is generally made to the atrocities committed by the British authorities on Asian and African people. The historical facts about the brutal ways in which the African people were enslaved, being herded like cattle and forcibly shipped to America, the West Indian islands and Latin America are conveniently not taught. Nor is there any mention of the similar way in which the British transported people from the Indian sub-continent to some parts of South America, the Caribbean, and later to East Africa to slave on their plantations and build their railways.

History is usually taught from a perspective that presents white people, and white culture, as civilised, and superior, and Black people and Black cultures as backward and inferior. So Asian students are taught in ways which tell them that their position in society has always been subordinate to that of white people. One white teacher was actually heard saying, 'Oh, these Black kids have only recently been freed from slavery and they really can't cope with all this freedom. They don't know what to do with it.'

In geography, there is the same assumption: that the 'Third World' is uncivilised and dependent on white generosity and cultural values. Even nowadays the text books always have pictures of Black people picking tea on plantations in India or Africa, inevitably with the white master in the foreground watching over them.

Nearly all images of Black people in school books are racist – 'golliwogs', 'uncivilised savages', and 'starving beggars' – and they are often sexist too. Black women and girls are either totally absent, or when they do appear, they are portrayed in very negative ways. The image of 'caring', but subservient, Afro-Caribbean woman, personifying motherhood and domesticity, is very common and has its roots in slavery – when, in fact, if women were not working on the plantations, they were responsible for caring for their white mistresses' children. The image is often of the Black mammy, or nurse, or domestic servant, ruling the kitchen with an 'iron glove'.

On the other hand, Asian women are portrayed as either sexually erotic or completely passive – dominated by their ruthless menfolk. These images are continually reinforced on television, in newspapers, magazines, and films, with Afro-Caribbean women nearly always in the role of nurses 'happily' performing menial tasks on hospital wards, while Asian women come across as pathetic, pitiful people, unable to speak English and understand what's going on around them, or, in contrast, beautiful air hostesses, serving and smiling at white men. The cumulative effect of all these images is to make Black people feel inferior, and correspondingly to make young whites more racist by giving them a sense of superiority.

Language is another major area of racist assumptions. Teachers often wrongly assume that Asian students are not fluent in English, and meanwhile schools place restrictions on the learning of Asian girls' own languages. As Ambreen says: ***If you're Asian, they automatically think your English is bad. The teachers don't consider that some white students also need English as a second language. I mean, I was born here, like the others, so I have always spoken English.***

In some schools English as a Second Language (ESL) is compulsory for most Asian students. Taira and Ambreen feel this isn't right, and as they point out: ***The teachers don't realise that we can speak two languages very well – our own mother tongue and English.*** Also Shada asks: ***If we have French and German options, why not other languages? It would help us. I would like to take an 'O' level in Gujerati.***

Some Muslim girls have insisted that they be allowed to wear shalwar (trousers) in schools, in keeping with their religion. It's often assumed that these girls are being pressured to wear shalwar by their parents, so that the school then takes on the role of the girls' saviour against their religion and tyrannical parents. In actual fact, the girls often want to wear them even when their parents are not bothered either way. In one case, girls organised a petition around their right to wear shalwar, culminating in a confrontation with the authorities. The girls emerged the winners.

When it comes to careers advice, some teachers regard the aspirations of Asian girls as stretching above what they can achieve – or beyond what they should ***expect*** as young Black women. When they do get advice, it very often directs them towards training in low status courses like state enrolled nursing, or into jobs like dress making, typing or domestic cleaning. Increasingly, young Black women are not even in a position to get these menial jobs because unemployment for Black school leavers is three times higher than for white students, and within this figure the unemployment rate is higher for young Black women than for men. The Youth Opportunities Programme (YOP), aimed at helping the young unemployed, is not free of racist and sexist assumptions: one YOP scheme supposed to be directed at the needs of Muslim girls, 'trained' them by taking them to work 'placements' where they participated by watching the young men digging old people's gardens.

Asian girls are well aware of being relegated to the worst paid jobs along with other Black people. Shashi said: ***People like us occupy the most unfavoured jobs which white people would not dream of doing, and whereas they might have the choice, we don't.*** Teachers often think that their Asian students' disappointment at not getting a decent job is their parents' fault for 'pushing' their daughters so hard. The responsibility is continually shifted away from the racism of institutions, like the schools, and individuals, like the teachers, onto the Asian parents.

Another issue is the distorted and often very wrong ideas that white teachers can hold about arranged marriages, which lead them to assume that Asian girls won't be allowed to go on to further education, or to the end of term party, or on school trips, because their parents might object to them mixing with boys. So, too often the girls themselves are not asked about their wishes, but just excluded from these activities.

Of course, there are some Asian parents who have objections, but there are some white parents who do too. The over-all stereotypical image of the Asian girl is that she is 'caught between two cultures', that of her parents, and that of her white friends. Asian girls are always presumed to be looking on enviously at their white friends going out to discos and films, and 'choosing' their own boyfriends . . . while they (poor things) are forced into marriage with someone twice their age who doesn't understand about romance like white men do, and whom they will not even see until the wedding ceremony.

But nobody seems to question the fact that the marriages of white girls are 'arranged', in that those who marry will do so with boys of a very similar class background, from the same area, and generally with their parents' consent. A white working class young woman who left school at sixteen, for example, has little or no chance of ***meeting*** (even if she wanted to) a white middle class boy at the local grammar school, let alone marrying one. The romantic notion of coming across Mr Right who just happens to cross your path is far from the reality of most young women's lives. And even when they do have some freedom of choice, what real freedom is there, as Pragna asks:

***Where is the freedom in going to a disco, frightened in case no boy fancies you, or no one asks you to dance, or your friends are walked home with boys and you have to walk home in the dark alone?***

And when Kamaljit and Rekha talk about their situations, it is clear that the stereotype doesn't hold very often and the horror stories are often distorted and exaggerated.

Kamiljit: ***I have known this boy for about two years now. We are not thinking of getting married yet, but if I was to tell my parents about it they would agree because he is my religion. Besides, all my sisters have married who they wanted, so I don't see why they should refuse me. My mum knows this boy, and she doesn't mind, but if he was English, I think she would mind. I don't know how she would react. She wouldn't be angry, but she would tell me not to see him. Then it would be up to me to decide whether to see him or not. But I am the sort who can't leave a family, but can leave a boy.***

Rekha: *My parents are all right because they let my sisters and I go anywhere we want to and come back when we like to. They're the same with my brother. It is all right as long as they know where we are and who we are with.*

Successive governments have used the notion of the Western 'romantic' marriage as being superior to other forms in order to bring in racist and sexist immigration, and now nationality, legislation. As part of his defence of the Nationality Bill, the Home Secretary Willie Whitelaw claimed to have received letters from Asian girls asking him to introduce restrictive legislation to keep out men who might be 'brought in' to marry them. But as Surjit points out: *The Government does not really give a damn as long as there are no more Black faces, they don't really mind who does what with their lives.*

Abida: *The main point is really to stop Black immigration and nought else. And the next thing they will say is 'Go home, we have no more use for you.'*

There is a growing confidence and awareness among many Asian girls about themselves and about their situations, especially in the climate of increased racist attacks on Black people, police harassment, and the growing number of white students being drawn into fascist organisations such as the British Movement and the National Front (and the newly formed New National Front) – all of whom try to recruit white school students. These Asian girls are continually challenging the passive image white people have had of them, and many are emerging as strong and militant young women.

*Pratibha Parmar, Nadira Mirza.*

# *Ageism in the Women's Liberation Movement*

We are two of the young women who are members of the ***Shocking Pink*** collective (***Shocking Pink*** is a magazine written and brought out by young women). Recently a group of us started talking seriously about ageism. This was sparked off by a conference report we read which said, 'We spoke of differences between ourselves in our late twenties and thirties and the younger lesbians coming into the movement.' Then crossed out, but still clearly visible, 'We wondered how deep their lesbianism was.' Obviously we were really angry. We tape recorded our discussion – here are some extracts.

– 'Generalisations are made all the time, just based on age, not taking that individual into account. You are judged on your age before you've even opened your mouth. I don't believe they'd make that ignorant assumption about class or race.'

– 'What can you do when you get a workshop full of women who are supposedly politically aware, who pat us on the head and tell us how wonderful ***Shocking Pink*** is, and then come up with a conclusion like, "We wonder how deep their lesbianism is"?'

Since becoming involved in the women's liberation movement, we'd often felt that in our relationships with a lot of older women there was something which made us feel uncomfortable, and when we thought about it more – shock, horror, dare we say it? – patronised. It wasn't until we started identifying ourselves as young women (which we only personally started to do when we got involved in ***Shocking Pink***) that we realised how we'd been identified or even classified by older women. By older, in this context, we mean anything as venerable as 24. We had already recognised our oppression as young women in the wider society – laws, parents, school and so on. But we hadn't realised we were also oppressed by older ***feminists***.

It was very nice to receive warmth and genuine support for ***Shocking Pink***. But most women said it was much more radical than they thought it would be – they had assumed that our politics would be wishy-washy and naive. Another popular fallacy was that we'd been given a lot of help from older women, because they didn't think we could have produced it on our own. Other women went over the top in the other direction, saying, 'Oh, you're so marvellous – this is wonderful!' Very nice . . . but in this context, such surprise is an insult.

It's offensive, because they seemed surprised that we ***could*** do it, rather than that we ***had***. And it also indicated that older women are totally out of touch with us and our politics. So no matter how much older feminists think it's important to put their energy into young women's projects, girls' nights in youth clubs and so on, it won't work if they see their role as educators. That's a patronising basis, neither equal nor conducive to trust.

What we are saying is that we already ***are*** feminists. There are at the moment many hundreds of young women, politically aware and active, defining their sexuality, organising women's groups in schools and colleges, forming bands, starting magazines. Your ageist assumptions deny us our ability to think for ourselves, to create and make our own decisions. In your minds, you place our feminism on another level, below that of yours.

Older women often tell us that we've had it easier, because they've fought the battles previously – like the one for women-only spaces. Of course, we acknowledge the gains you've already made – but that doesn't automatically mean that things are easier for us. We have other struggles, which perhaps you didn't have to face – like being beaten up at school by skinheads for wearing a dyke badge. We can get expelled for calling the headmaster sexist, suspended for wearing trousers, or dyeing our hair, or labelled a deviant and troublemaker – ruining our educational chances – because of our feminist views.

We've ***all*** got it hard. We must stop turning it into some kind of competition, and recognise each other's struggles.

These views, that it's older women who have made it all possible for us, tend to go hand in hand with some kind of assumption that we've learnt our feminism from an older feminist – a feminist mother, sister, teacher. Nobody we know has a feminist mother . . . most of us have ***sought out*** the women's movement, with some considerable difficulty. It doesn't exactly reach out and grab you, especially if you live in the provinces, or are Black, or are working class.

In fact, at first, when we did find the women's movement most of us were completely intimidated by the structure and jargon. Even 'ageism' – what kind of word is that? It's taken some time for us to learn our 'isms' from our 'ists'. We sat for six months in meetings with our mouths shut. We were forced to learn the political language of feminism. What this means in real terms is the exclusion of all the women who just don't have access to the knowledge of this language.

It's much the same with codes of dress, the significance of adopting certain styles. We have ***different*** influences – things change in ten years – and our ***own*** styles, but we feel that these are often misinterpreted by older women. There is an accepted code of dress among feminists and we are sometimes regarded with suspicion if we don't conform to it. For instance, if we turn up at a party wearing 'frivolous' clothes, the equation may be made that frivolous clothes equal frivolous politics.

When we started to challenge older women about their ageism, we were amazed and disappointed at the reactions we got. We found that lip-service was paid to the idea of respecting or acknowledging the presence and politics of young women. They say 'young women' – never 'girl', or if they do they say 'girls are powerful'. We feel that this language,although correct, is a token measure, unless it is backed up by a true understanding of ageism, which we feel is often lacking, as, when confronted, a lot of women seem to think it is all a bit of a joke. At the risk of appearing humourless, let us assure you that it's no joke to be told by someone who can hardly hold back an amused and indulgent smile at your naiveté that she really doesn't know what you're making so much fuss about.

It's true that a lot of women genuinely haven't considered their ageism, and do try to change when it's pointed out. But just as many see it as complaining, or rebelling, in a 'typically adolescent way', and assume that once we've reached the dizzy heights of twenty, we'll look back smiling at how important it all seemed at the time. In other words, the problem of ageism keeps getting glossed over because all of those Angry Young Women will soon grow into 'responsible' adults, and will probably start smiling indulgently at a few young women themselves.

It was hard to understand this ageism at first. How come women who've suffered from ageism become ageist themselves? The answer seems to be that ageism towards the young is a relatively recently named oppression. There have never been, until recently, a lot of teenage feminists, and because most women came to feminism in their early twenties or later, they didn't have a political consciousness at the time they were experiencing ageism, and they were unable to identify it as such.

We know that ageism is also suffered by women over 40, in different forms and in different ways. But we couldn't define some other group's oppression – that's not up to us, though of course we support them. In our society, there seems to be a perfect age. Women seem to be working on the assumption that age equals maturity – an idea we don't agree with. We feel that 'maturity' is a very ambiguous and misused term anyway.

It's often asked, 'Where are all the young women to take up the struggle?' Well . . . why should we join something where we are dismissed on so many levels? Women often seem to doubt our commitment, thinking we'll give it up for a pair of roller skates next week. At some point, you'll just have to learn to trust us. If you'd ever listened properly to us, you'd know those fears were unfounded. ***You*** are perpetuating the division between us.

The women's movement must now come to terms with the contradiction of needing young women to be part of it, and treating us as if we were smaller, inadequate and immature versions of the older women in it. Obviously our experiences are different from yours. But that doesn't make them less valid. Aren't we all meant to be learning from each other, and sharing these experiences? We can never really be together until the oppression of ageism is recognised and worked on.

*Sally and Ilona*

## *An afterword to this book*

It really struck us just how much anger there was with older people in nearly all the pieces in this book. But this oppression by older people was never named as ageism – except in one piece on the Age of Consent. It was often not considered as important as sexism, racism and classism. Ageism is so deep as to be invisible.

The book itself is an example of the control older women have over our lives. Edited by older women, all pieces have had to be approved by both the ***Spare Rib*** and the ***Sheba*** collectives, neither of which contain young women. This raises the obvious question, why? The unwillingness of older people to give up their power means that we are dependent on their good will to be given a space to discuss our oppression publicly.

It's good that this book gives us this space, and it will be useful if it causes older women to examine and change their attitudes. It won't have achieved much if you read it and just think, 'How sweet'. Although it hasn't been named in most of the pieces in a 'political' language, the consciousness of ageism is there throughout – and the actions and experiences described are a challenge to the way you see us.

*Sally and Ilona*

# *Helpful information and contacts*

**MEN'S AND JNG WOMEN'S ƆUPS**

If you want to know if there's a women's liberation group in your area you can write (with a stamped addressed envelope) to one of the following, or ring them up:
*A Woman's Place*, 48 William IV Street, London WC2 (01 836 6081)
*WIRES* (Women's Information Referral and Enquiry Service), 32a Shakespeare Street, Nottingham (0602 411475)
(Please note – if you buy this book a while after it's been published, addresses and phone numbers may have changed. If you get no reply, check with *Spare Rib*.)
Or you can advertise free in *Spare Rib*, in the classified ads sections, either to say you've formed a group, or to find others to form one with. Write to *Spare Rib* Classifieds.

**ORMATION ON JAL RIGHTS AND ORTUNITIES IN IOOLS/COLLEGES**

*Advisory Centre for Education:* 18 Victoria Park Square, London E2 (01 980 4596)
*CASSOE* (Campaign against Sexism and Sexual Oppression in Education): c/o Liz Wynton, 17 Lymington Road, London NW6.
*NAME* (National Association for Multi Racial Education): 86 Station Rd, Mickleover, Derby (0332 511751)
*Equal Opportunities Commission*, (EOC): Overseas House, Quay St, Manchester 3 (061 833 9244)
*National Council for Civil Liberties*: 21 Tabard St, London, SE1 (01 403 3888)
*Scottish Council for Civil Liberties*: 146 Holland St, Glasgow 2 (041 332 5960)
*National Union of Teachers*: c/o Women's Official, Hamilton House, Mabledon Place, London WC1 (01 387 2442)
*Women in the National Union of Teachers (WiNUT)*: c/o Jan Pollock, 25 Highgate West Hill, London N6 (01 348 2888)
*Women in Education* (also publish newsletter): 24 St Brendans Rd, Manchester 20.
*Sheffield Women in Education*: c/o Hunter House Rd, Sheffield 11
*Children's Legal Centre* 2 Malden Road, London NW5 (01 267 6392)
*National Union of Students*: Women's Rights Group, 3 Endsleigh St, London WC1 (01 387 1277)
*National Union of School Students*: c/o Poly of Central London, Students Union, 104-108 Bolsover Street, London W1 (01 636 6271)
*Useful books*: *First Rights*, published by NCCL (see above), from them for £1.25. And many useful booklets from EOC (see above). For details of how to get catalogue of feminist

books in general, send stamped addressed envelope to Sisterwrite Bookshop, 190 Upper Street, London N1. Open Tues — Sat

**YOUTH ORGANISATIONS**

With resources and support for work with girls and young women

*National Association of Youth Clubs*, c/o Girls Project Officer, 30 Peacock Lane, Leicester (0533 29514). Publishes newsletter on *Working With Girls*, resource pack, and will inform on girl's work projects/centres in all areas.

*National Youth Bureau*, 17-23 Albion St, Leicester (0533 554775). Also advises on working with girls.

**SEXUALITY**

*Brook Advisory Centres*: advice for young women on birth control, personal problems, sexuality and abortion. Head Office (will advise on other area offices) 153a East Street, London SE17 (01 1234 or 1390)

*National Abortion Campaign*: 374 Grays Inn Rd, London WC (01 278 0153) fights for a woman's right to choose. Will put you in touch with your local campaign group.

*Family Planning Information Service*: 27-35 Mortimer Stree (01 636 7866), will advise on clinics nationally, and which have youth advisory clinics.

*Young Lesbians Group*: c/o Camden Girls Project, 4 Caversham Rd, London NW5 (01 267 2898)

*Lesbian Line*: (telephone help, information, support) in many areas – details from London Lesbian Line Mon and Fri 2-10pm, Tues-Thurs 7-10pm (01 837 8602)

**PUBLICATIONS**

*Shocking Pink*: magazine produced by young women's collective. Information from – and contributions to – c/o Cromer St Women's Centre, Cromer St, London WC1.

*Working with Girls Newsletter*: see National Association of Youth Clubs, above.

*Women in Education Newsletter*: see Women in Education, above.

*Women in NUT Newsletter*: see Women in NUT, above.

*Spare Rib*: 27 Clerkenwell Close, London EC1 (01 253 9792

Several girls' projects (youth clubs) bring out their own publications – for details, contact National Association of Clubs, as above.

**HOW TO GET SPARE RIB**

*On sale in newsagents*, local and chain. If they don't have it, please tell them it's distributed by COMAG, and ask them to order it for you.

*Become a subscriber*. Rates for individuals: £8 for 12 copie a year, posted to your home. (Six month subscription for

individuals £4.50). Rates for institutions (libraries etc): £12
Write to ***Spare Rib*** subscriptions.
***Group order***. For sales at women's groups, at work, college, school, etc. Five copies or more monthly (can stop during school/college holidays), at discount, sale or return.
Write to ***Spare Rib*** Direct Sales.
***For free sample copy*** – if you've never seen Spare Rib, but would like to try one, write to ***Spare Rib*** GAP Sample.
*Spare Rib,* 27 Clerkenwell Close, London EC1 OAT.

## *Credits and acknowledgements*

Pieces in this collection previously published as follows

LOOKS: Penny Sillin, Bert's New Image, Cindy, all from ***Shocking Pink*** 2; Bovver boots ***Spare Rib*** 93; One small horrid word SR89, 92; Trousers, SR89.

AT SCHOOL: Women's Libber SR75; To school with fear SR62; Acting it out SR85; Oh ma gawd SR75; Soft and soppy SR75; The box up SR75; This book is for boys SR75; Bores, snobs, breakdowns SR99; When you give up SR110.

AT HOME: Young, broke, stuck at home SR98; The Pandemonium SR100; Down the plughole SR104; A day in the life SR65; It's a boy's life SR112. Photos see below.

AT WORK: Electrical engineer SR48; Hairdressing and Shop work Saturdays to be published SR; Babysitting SR106; Out of School onto the Dole SR107; General Maid SR44.

FRIENDS AND LOVERS: Teenage sexism SR2; A girl's best friend SR58; Unlawful sex SR108; Love and romance SR82; Confessions SR115; Forced to deceive SR39; Protection racket SR108; Going out with boys to be published SR; Pressure, problems SR108. Photos see below.

TOGETHER: Perspex, Youth clubs; Such a relief SR95; No more chaos SR95; Growing angry SR111; Ageism in the WLM not published elsewhere. Photos see below.

PHOTOGRAPHS: The young women on pages 67, 68, 99, 100, 119, 120, 133 and 141 were photographed (in colour) by Anita Corbin, between August 1980 and April 1981 for a third year photo arts project at the Polytechnic of Central London. 'As a young woman myself, I wanted to look at our visual identities, because I felt there was a lack of photos showing our actual life styles.' It's now become part of a travelling exhibition called ***Visible Girls***, based at the Cockpit Arts Workshop and available for hire or loan, phone 01 405 5334.

Photos on pages 53 and 75 by Dianne Ceresa.
Photo on page 142 by Val Wilmer.

ILLUSTRATIONS: Penny Sillin by Sue; Bert's New Image by Monica; Cindy by Nelly Spit and Sue Bong. Cartoon page 15, Lisa Bahaire. Drawings pages 20 and 33, Caroline Jackson. Cartoon, page 40, Liz Mackie. The Box Up, girl students, Hertfordshire primary school.

COVER: design and lettering by Pat Kahn, photos by Dianne Ceresa.

## *Sheba Feminist Publishers*

Sheba is a feminist publishing cooperative, formed in March 1980. All our books are available by mail order from Sheba, 488 Kingsland Road, London E8. Please add 30p per volume for p&p. Write for our catalogue of books, cards and posters.

## *Other books are*

*Sour Cream*, Jo Nesbitt, Liz Mackie, Lesley Ruda, Christine Roche. A collection of feminist cartoons, 2nd edition. £1.25.

*The Ten-Woman Bicycle*, Tricia Vita. Illustrations by Marion Crezée. A charming story about how women enter a 'man's world' – together. Particularly suited to children. £1.25.

*Woman and Russia*, translated and with an introduction by the Birmingham-based Women and Eastern Europe group. The first feminist samizdat, published in Leningrad in December 1979 and immediately suppressed. This is its first appearance in English. £1.95.

*Smile, smile, smile, smile*, Alison Fell, Ann Oosthuizen, Stef Pixner, Tina Reid, Michele Roberts. A collection of feminist poetry and short stories illustrated with drawings by the writers. 'As my moods change from elation to self-irony to depression and back again, I find poems here to comfort and affirm my experiences'. *Feminist Review*. £1.75

*Feminist Fables*. Suniti Namjoshi. Drawings by Susan Trangmar. An elegant and subversive collection of stories that rework mythology as it *used* to be . . . they create an uniquely feminist pattern of meaning. £2.25.

*Spitting the Pips Out*, Gillian Allnutt. As if entries in a notebook, painful, humourous, despairing, hopeful, this collection of poems, prose and wry comments tell the story of one woman's journey towards selfhood. Though the story is autobiographical, many women will recognise it as their own. £2.25.

*Loneliness and Other Lovers*, Ann Oosthuizen. A novel of changes, heartaches and discoveries as Jean ceases to be 'someone's wife' and builds her own life, for herself. £2.75.

*The Great Escape of Doreen Potts*, Jo Nesbitt. An irreverent children's book written and illustrated by feminist cartoonist Jo Nesbitt, with sturdy heroine Doreen outwitting everyone in their attempts to marry her off to the stupid prince. £2.50

***For Ourselves***, Anja Meulenbelt. A radical new look at women's sexuality (translated from the Dutch). Richly illustrated with photographs and cartoons, the book is a joyful celebration of who we really are, what we really look like, dismissing once and for all the passive Playboy image that has for so long been called our sexuality. £4.50.

***Sour Cream 2***. A new collection by thirteen feminist cartoonists: provocative, hilarious, thought provoking. £1.75.

***Our Own Freedom***, Maggie Murray. Introduction by Buchi Emeche ta. 'These photographs of women in Africa show that the basic things of life – obtaining water, fire, shelter, the care of the young and the sick – are almost entirely done by women. These are the basic necessities of life and yet there is little or no compensation to the women who do them. Because they are unpaid, such tiring and boring chores are called 'women's work.' These words come from Buchi Emecheta's introduction to Maggie Murray's photographs of women in Africa. £3.75